Collected Poems

Gaberbocchus Press

By the same author

Professor Mmaa's Lecture
Bayamus
Cardinal Pölätüo
Wooff Wooff
Tom Harris
General Piesc
The Mystery of the Sardine
Hobson's Island

Logic Labels and Flesh
Factor T
Special Branch
On Semantic Poetry
Semantic Divertissements
The Chair of Decency

Apollinaire's Lyrical Ideograms
Jankel Adler
Kurt Schwitters in England

Dno Nieba

St. Francis & the Wolf of Gubbio

The Adventures of Peddy Bottom

Stefan Themerson
Collected Poems

with drawings by Franciszka Themerson

Gaberbocchus

© Stefan Themerson Estate 1997
First published January 1998
Reprinted July 1998
Gaberbocchus Press/De Harmonie
P.O. Box 3547, 1001 AH Amsterdam
ISBN 9061693977
Printed in Holland by Hooiberg, Epe

Distributed in the U.S., Canada and the United Kingdom
by the Overlook Press.
ISBN 0-87951-846-4

England, table, Hamlet and I
got ~~cooked~~ scrambled together ~~and~~ with minus π
~~What skill will manage to pull them apart~~ who
Politics? Logic? Science? or Art?

Who'll be fit to pull

What skill will be able to pull them
                                    apart
                            have
Whom shall we ask to pull them
                    get   apart,
Who will you have to pull them
    huds in may   apart

CONTENTS

preface 9

poems 15

index of first lines 157

index of titles 169

list of illustrations 171

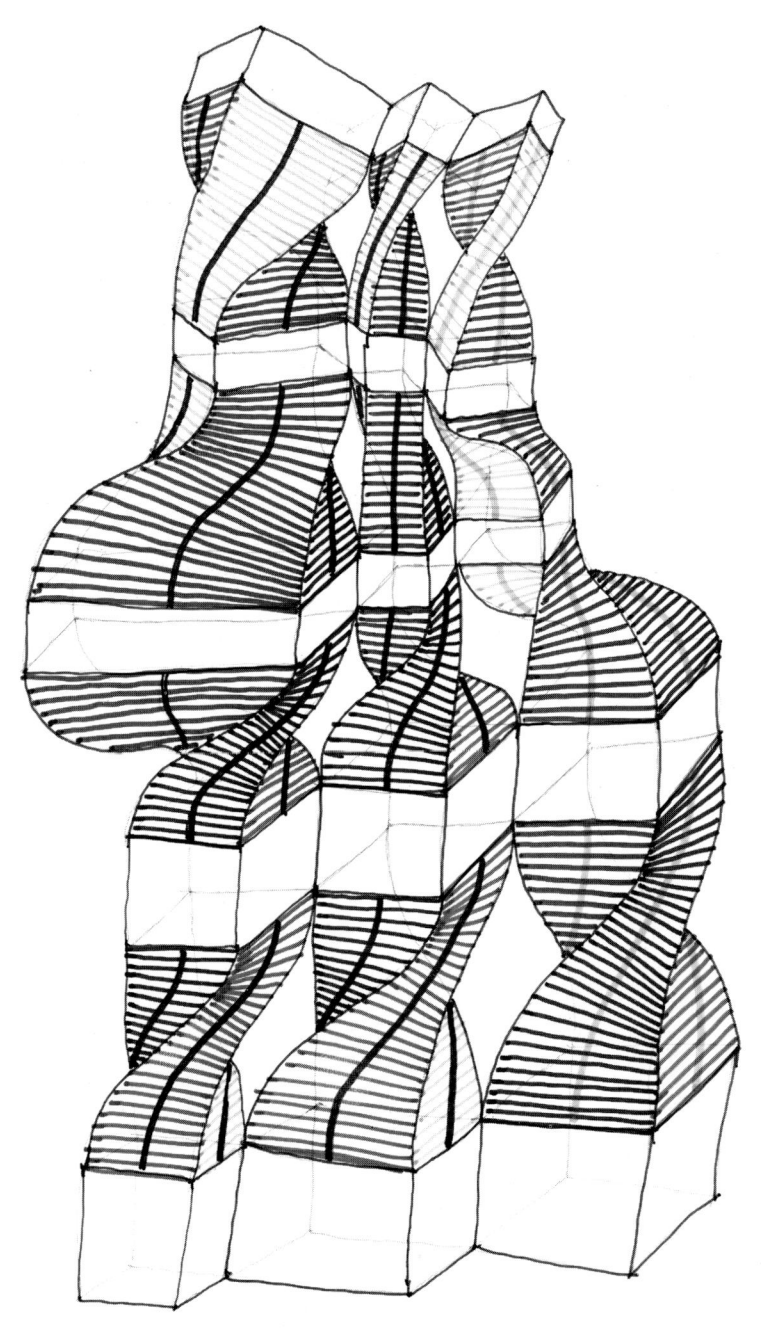

am I treble?
(body, mind, I)

Stefan Themerson

PREFACE

This volume contains almost all of the poems Stefan Themerson wrote in English, spanning the years 1942 to 1988, when he lived in London. There is one exception, the eight-part poem, *Croquis dans les Ténèbres*, which was written in France in 1941. It is published here for the first time in its entirety, in Barbara Wright's English translation.

Stefan Themerson wrote poems since his student days, while he was making films, when writing novels and throughout the time he ran the Gaberbocchus Press, which he founded with his wife, the artist Franciszka Themerson, in 1948. His earliest poems were published when he was seventeen in a local newspaper of his native town, Płock in Poland. They were already distinguished by wit, an imaginative use of language and a pleasure in paradox. Up to 1937 his poems were written in Polish. Some were for children, and were accompanied by Franciszka's illustrations. After the move to Paris in 1937, Stefan Themerson continued to write in Polish but within a year was also writing in French and making translations of his Polish poems.

His longest, and perhaps most ambitious poem, *Croquis dans les Ténèbres*, was written during the war in France and originally published in England in French. It was printed privately in 1944 and distributed by Hachette in London. He started writing this poem in Marseille and continued in Voiron where he spent most of 1941, living at the Hôtel de la Poste, a Red Cross shelter for Polish soldiers whose regiments had been disbanded.

After his arrival in England in 1942, he continued to translate his poems, this time into English, often in several versions with many minor changes. He was impatient with the limitations of translation and with the constraints it imposed on precise expression.

> If only those few words
> that are used in poetry
> could rhyme in all
> languages.

The frustration of crossing the boundaries of language in translation inspired a short-lived experiment with trilingual poems, early in this volume. But Themerson soon turned to other ways of extending poetic possibilities. In 1945 he started working on a new form of translation which exposed the limitations of conventional poetic nuance and the subterfuge of local colour. He called it Semantic Poetry—a sort of poetry which strips language of all its associations and rids it of the redundant debris that clings to words and sentences, obscuring and disguising their meaning.

Semantic Poetry makes its first appearance in *Bayamus*, published by Poetry London in 1949, when the three-legged hero, Bayamus, becomes intent on discovering the 'real naked truth' of a French song.

> 'I knew now'—thought Bayamus to himself—'that the best way of discovering it, was to throw away the mystificatory aureolas of conventional, traditional, patriotic, artistic, moral, customary, *couleur locale* associations, to do it by replacing the words of the song with definitions from emotionally neutral dictionary words, rigorously accurate, conforming closely to required standards of precision.'[1]

A prototypical example of Semantic Poetry is at the beginning of the second movement of the Semantic Sonata, p. 99.

> What is ceiling for my neighbour downstairs
> is floor for me
> How can we ever find one another
> if
> unwilling
> to replace words by terms
> and to call it: Horizontal structure of wood or other material
> dividing storeys of a building.

---

[1] *Bayamus*, p. 46

Semantic Poetry is an attitude of mind. It is a method of disposing of ambiguity and precluding any possibility of reading between the lines. But it was Stefan Themerson's conviction that there was never a single way of doing anything, and Semantic Poetry, even if it informed all of his work, in poetry and in prose, was just one possibility.

His Semantic Poetry translations of existing poems/songs, have been published several times since 1945, but *On Semantic Poetry*, Gaberbocchus, 1975, includes the final versions of them all.

In this collection, the poems follow a roughly chronological order, An exact chronological sequence would have been difficult to achieve, partly because Stefan Themerson rarely dated his poems and partly because versions often co-exist, having been worked and re-worked over a period of years. It seemed best to arrange a sequence which flows naturally from one idea to another, or from one form to another.

Occasionally, Themerson would take a section of a poem out of its original context and give it a different title or a different arrangement. This is the case with some parts of the SEMANTIC SONATA. The first part of the SONATA, for instance, has been published in its separate incarnation as: *Since the first Day of Genesis*. The part which begins: 'Sugar is soluble in water...' appears elsewhere as A ROUNDELAY *on the Narrowness and Unexpandability of Words*. The Recapitulation of the 4th Movement also appears as a separate poem, and is the subject of two further variations, one on philosophy and one on truth, which are not included here. *The Aim of Aims* is the actual title of only one of the poems but as a theme it occurs in several others, including *You asked me to read to you...*, which is an introduction to a poetry reading—sometimes treated as a poem, sometimes as prose. The index of first lines, on page 157, lists the poems in all of their configurations.

Most of the poems are published here for the first time. Some were obviously intended for publication, having been typed in what was clearly a final version. Some had been included by Stefan Themerson in a special selection kept for his poetry readings. Others came to light, after his death in 1988, as casually hand-written drafts, some with several variants, none of which may have been the final version.

The earliest poems in Polish were in rhyme, as were a few of those in French, but almost none in English. The evolution of the English poems proceeded slowly, over a period of 45 years, from complex to simpler structures and themes, and from an emotional tone to epigrammatic wisdom. Language is always treated as a precise material, strong and delicate, with which one can equally well construct edifices and seed clouds.

The process of writing poetry is itself often the subject. Other recurrent themes are verbal misunderstandings, philosophical pitfalls and good manners. There are mirror images, reflections and repetitions. There are repetitions which allow the mind to find new meanings in a familiar repertoire. There are verbal repetitions which build up to a new structure and new meaning. There are formal repetitions and thematic repetitions. There are also versions—sometimes several—of a single poem, or a single version with several alternative titles. The reader will soon recognise the Themersonian repertoire.

A few poems were accompanied by pictures in their original publication. Wherever possible, the same pictures, drawn by Franciszka Themerson, have been included here.

This is the first volume of Stefan Themerson's works to be prepared for publication since his death in 1988 and without his personal involvement. It is also the first extensive collection of his poems to be published. A guiding influence in its preparation has been the thought of how he might have done it himself.

I am grateful for the encouragement of Jaco Groot of Gaberbocchus Press in Amsterdam, and Bernard Stone of the Turret Bookshop in London, with its permanent celebration of Themersoniana until its closure in 1994. I am enormously indebted to Nick Wadley for his unstinting help in preparing the material; to Barbara Wright, who as well as translating *Croquis*, read and advised on all of the poems, and to Klara Kopcińska who uncovered many of them, when working on the Themerson archive.

Jasia Reichardt

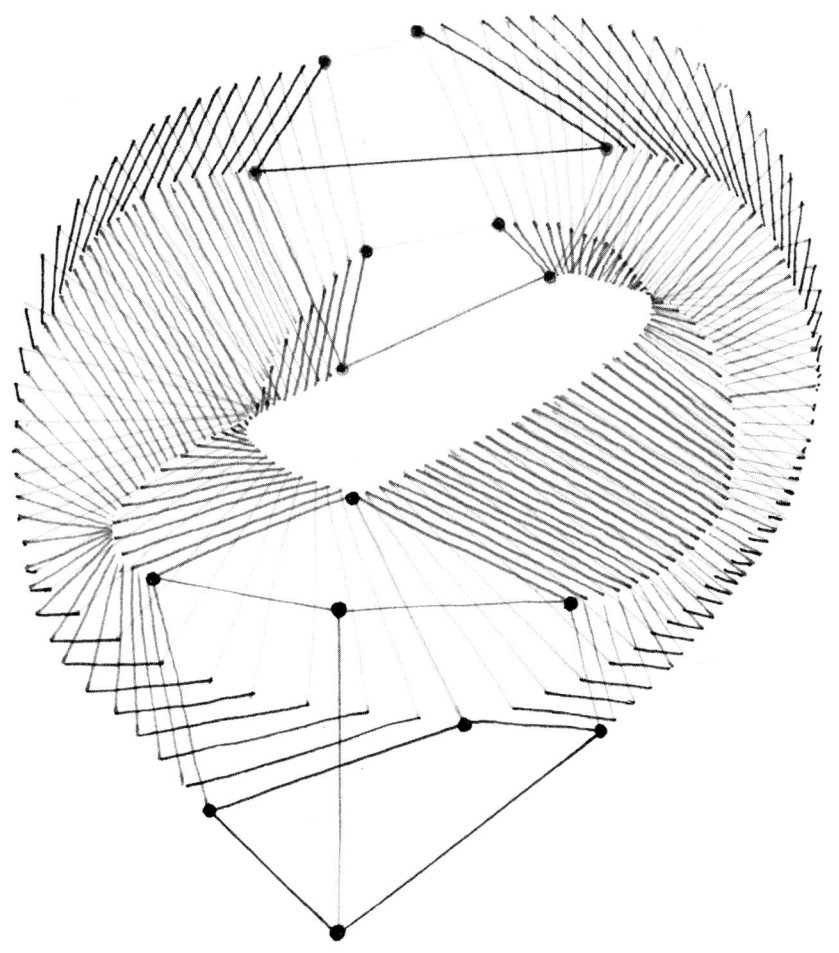

CROQUIS DANS LES TÉNÈBRES
translated by Barbara Wright

Petit Nègre Ecrire Petit Poème
Croquis dans les Ténèbres
I
II
III
IV
V
VI
Grecian Night

PETIT NÈGRE ÉCRIRE PETIT POÈME

I am a poor child abandoned by the Muses. They've gone up the marble staircase, the cloud-staircase, and they've climbed higher towards *On High*, while I've been left down here, all alone.

It's true, the Heavens begin where the earth stops being hard and palpable, they start a quarter of a millimetre above the pavements and the grass. Yes, I too am immersed in the Ocean of the Heavens, but I move through it as the crab moves through the sea—with its claws. It's because my soles and heels are stuck in the bed of the Ocean of the Heavens that I've been left down here, where I was born.

Why did you lose patience, oh my Muses, why did you flee, why didn't you wait until the end of the war?

I've been left all alone with my pencil and a glass of wine—so much has happened around me in thirty long years that I can neither remember it, nor draw any conclusions, nor find any common denominator. Because I've lost the strength of strong men, of magnificent men, of monster-men, who have their own warlike will; because I don't want to be a man like them; because I am a poor, abandoned child.

But after a glass of wine, the things we're talking about emerge of their own accord from their strange shells, like snails after rain, and begin their sleepwalk. Alas, the poet's body stays behind, the Muses have fled, but he must stay where his soles and heels are.

Oh, you Engineers! You have measured the surface of the earth, you have divided these two numbers, and you have said: 'But there's an enormous amount of land, there's plenty of space for people to walk where they will, there's enough room for everyone to give free rein to all his fantasies.' But there you are—you've been counting on the logic of counting. And yet we haven't anywhere to sleep, we haven't anywhere to escape to, we haven't anywhere to move around, or even to stand.

And that's why we can't stay within the two dimensions of the surface of the earth, and why we want to escape to *On High*. But our soles and our heels are stuck to the pavements and the Muses have abandoned our space, and wine costs a hundred sous a litre.

So where is the Celestial Grocer who would sell us a litre of poetry? I'm going to look for him, with a lantern in my thirsty hands, I'm going to look for him in far-off, eternal worlds, and in the corners of my mortal room.

But he's hiding in invisible holes, which are camouflaged by the black depths of our time. And the only hope is that he has built up some stocks, and that the time will come when he'll release them, to fill our poor sentimental shops.

I am all alone with my angel—who is no more.

CROQUIS DANS LES TÉNÈBRES

I

'Come on, hand it over, Sebastian, Sebastian!'

And Sebastian, surprised, astonished, thinks:
'What do they want me to hand over?'

'Come on, hand it over, Sebastian!'... so much conviction in their voices, but Sebastian really doesn't know what they want.

The calm surface of the lake ripples and quivers—but no more than is necessary to show that it's alive.

Above the surface: the sky, and clouds much lighter than the sky, like clouds in photos taken through a yellow filter.

But on the bank, between the landing stage and the shore, in a dark gully, the olive-green water is a stagnant, motionless mass, here and there glinting when touched by the light. It is only on the surface that things are reflected: the rotting boards of the landing stage, the stony shore, the sloping deck; but just scratch this surface picture and what will immediately appear—not to your eyes but to your nostrils and your mouth and your fingers—are the dark, humid, stinking depths where rats are swimming on their backs.

And suddenly that ham actor Cucynski shows up. He goes and straddles the gully of stagnant water, he leans over it and looks into its depths, he smiles quite pleasantly, now and then glancing around him.

He's got nicely tanned the last few days, walking along the mule tracks, since he was for ever out walking between his rare auditions; while he walked he would be eating, gossiping, intriguing—living, in other words... pah! he looked as if he was going for a walk even when he was on the stage, where he was supposed to be someone quite different from Cucynski.

He went walking without a hat on his naked head that he doesn't have shaved any more; and his short black hair is growing, and twists and turns, still very timidly, in little tufts, as if it didn't know that one day it would be allowed to lie flat, quietly and soberly, on either side of a parting.

Is it possible that Cucynski thinks that Sebastian has hidden some mysterious object in the water? That he has grabbed a sunbeam, wrapped it round a spool, and thrown it into the bottom of the lake?

'Hand it over, Sebastian, we've had enough...'

'But what is it you want? tell me!'

They shut their ears, though. They just can't imagine that he doesn't know. They think Sebastian is teasing them, and they ask once again:

'Hand it over!'

Then Sebastian brings his hand up to the inside pocket of his jacket and he feels a handful of warm air in his palm.

This is an unexpected discovery. He's afraid to look... he holds his hand under his jacket and with the tips of his fingers he h e a r s the acute trembling of a little yellow beak, and the tickling of the down.

Then he grasps this handful of warmth more tightly, and brings it out of the twilight of his breast into the middle of the aerial landscape, suspended over the surface of the lake.

'Is this what you're talking about? Friends!'

They look at each other, themselves astonished. But there is so much candour in his question that they suddenly realize that he really didn't know what he had to hand over, what they were asking for. And, simultaneously, they realize that they themselves don't know what they want, either, or rather, that they can't imagine what form this 'thing' they are expecting should take.

Is this little chick the form of their desires? Their hearts take fright, and they look Sebastian up and down as if he were a conjuror, and once again they don't know—perhaps he's still teasing them?

The little chick is in Sebastian's palm as if it were in a tiny nest, and they are afraid that the chick might really be the form of their desires, they fear the quivering reality of the chick. Sebastian feels their agitation, and he hides the little bird in his breast.

A flag has been hoisted above the landing stage. It flutters in the wind with its gaily-coloured zigzag, and it's the only bright spot in the opaline air that fills all space. In the middle of the lake there is a sailing dinghy whose mainsail is the colour of the cloud hanging above it in the sky. Everything that is, is in nature: the sail, and Sebastian, and the questions and the answers.

The little chick, snug in the warmth inside his jacket, has melted into Sebastian's body. Sebastian holds out his arms, and, without a word, hugs his friends. There is no Cucynski among them; he's still straddling the stagnant gully, smiling vaguely and examining the water. Sebastian embraces his friends.

And then, suddenly—have they discovered something? have they become wiser?—they understood that their cry of 'Come on, hand it over, Sebastian, Sebastian!' would have been tactless, had it not been childishly naive.

Despite the famine, the chick wasn't eaten.

II

'I can't get used to...'—he fell silent. He sat down on the windowsill and glanced inside the room.

In this room there was a terrifying reality, and he knew he couldn't touch it, because the real fingers of an angel can't grasp a void that is so sparsely filled with atoms; the fingers of angels are hard, and they can't get a hold on the void that is called matter.

In this room there was a woman, a woman lying on a bed, a woman covered with a blanket pulled right up to her closed eyes.

In this room there was a mirror in a gilt frame, and this mirror reflected the woman on the bed.

In this room there was a table with a glass of water.

In this room the lamp was lit; had the woman forgotten to put it out? had she been afraid to fall asleep in the dark?

It was not because of the light of the lamp that all of this existed, but because of his eyes. Because in the room itself there was no image. They were only in the angel's eyes, the images of the room, of the bed, of the woman, of the mirror, of the table, of the lamp. It may perhaps be difficult to imagine without light, but nowhere are there any images without eyes.

'It's too little: if I had different eyes,' said the angel, 'the world would look different to me. It would be different. Because the world is what I see.' And the angel, rather pleased with this profound philosophical thought, got down from the windowsill and went his way, along the street but high, high up above the road, as if he were walking along an invisible tram wire overhead.

But there weren't any trams in the town. The streets were empty, and the only living things were the houses, examining one another with their half-open windows.

And the angel sat down on the windowsills, and he kept glancing through the windows, and he shrank back in horror at the empty matter piling up in the rooms; often he clung convulsively to the window frames so as not to lose his balance, and he quickly retreated to the middle of the street, high up above the road, his head on the moonlit roofs.

But, attracted once again by the rectangular breach in the wall, he went back to it in order to look o u t s i d e f r o m t h e e x t e r i o r. And suddenly he found himself face to face with the man who was looking at the sky. The man was a poet, but he wasn't looking at the sky to find in the moon, as enigmatic as all nature, the inspiration to write a poem, a sentimental love poem. The sky was much more than that, for him.

He looked out of the window and he knew that with his fingers, which were made of empty matter, he couldn't grasp—he could never get hold of—the hardness of the abstraction outside the window, which lives implacably outside matter.

The man sat down on the windowsill and suddenly shrank back, terrified by the hardness of his own thoughts—it is they that are 'abstraction'; he clung convulsively to the window frame, because he was feeling giddy and he didn't want to lose his balance and fall down on to the pavement below; he quickly retreated to the middle of his room, but soon went back to the window and again sat down on the sill.

And then he found himself face to face with the angel, who was looking into the room. They stared at each other for a long, long time; they stared at each other in a friendly fashion.

It was the man who spoke first:

'Tell me', he began, 'what happens when someone has gone through the window? Is it true that he falls like a stone to the pavement, and that that's all?'

'Oh no', replied the angel. 'That won't be all. At the same time you'll become quite real, you'll grow real wings, and all the angels will be able to touch you with their real, hard fingers... I assure you', he added, in some embarrassment, 'it isn't particularly interesting.'

The man stared at the angel for a very long, long time, as if he wanted to read his eyes: was he speaking sincerely?

And then it was the angel who asked:
'And you too—will you tell me what happens after you've gone through the window?
'Is it true that you become petrified, that you're transformed into winged stone, such as you see in the cemeteries of museums, and that that's all?'

'Oh no', replied the man. 'That won't be all. At the same time you'll become quite real. You'll become so real, as real as I am, that every man will be able to touch you with his fingers, and he *will* touch you, and there will even be too many of them who'll be touching you.'

The angel stared at the man for a very long, long time, as if he wanted to read his eyes: was he telling the truth?

Then the man pointed to the back of the room where a woman was lying on a bed, covered right up to her closed eyes.

The angel looked at the blanket and he noticed an enormous swelling where her big, pregnant belly was.

Somewhere up above, the clouds were gliding. The squall fell, trapped in the street below. The yellowish street lamps were beginning to reveal the twilight.

The lace curtain quivered, like the surface of a lake, and at that moment the window closed of its own accord.

For a very long, long time, they stared at each other through the transparent window pane, the man and the angel—who was no other than the man's thought.

And then they laid both their hands, the left and the right, on the surfaces of the window pane, and between their hands they pressed their warm lips on the cool glass, and they kissed the two sides of the same thing.

The clouds were racing each other beneath the moon and, on the earth, chasing their own sharp, shapeless shadows.

The man and the angel-his-thought turned away from the window, and each went his own way.

III

I never believed in Thee, God,
so Thou owest me nothing.
But what about those who have gone to churches,
    chapels, synagogues, mosques
—they are the ones to whom Thou must give
a chunk of bread buttered with freedom,
a slice of bread covered with a radiant smile of independence,
—they are the ones to whom Thou must give
a little wing of thine angel in a soup plate of the clearest
    of clear soups.

They have earned this by the sweat of their brow
    in thine enigmatic workshops,
and by their slaves' tears,
and by their services at thine altars.

Here I am, I appear before Thee as the impostor of an emissary,
    as an unbidden, sad go-between.
Wouldst Thou be the God of anaemic women,
wouldst Thou be the God of the tuberculous,
    of those pale, wandering shadows
        who gasp for breath when climbing the stairs.
Art Thou already so distant from thy radiant Hellenic ideal?

Oh, God of Abraham, of Isaac and of Jacob,
God of Jan, of Jean and of Juan,
God of Ivan, of Johann and of John!
Oh, totem! Oh, mana! Oh, taboo!
Oh, impersonal, omnipresent force, both material and spiritual,
Oh, immortal and eternal Bun-Jil, who hast regulated the course
    of the sun and the moon,
Oh, moral God, oh Varuna, who watchest over the world and guidest
    humanity,
Oh, Aton, thou who carest for men's maintenance, and who givest
    them the nourishment they crave,
Oh, chain of cause and effect of an Alexander of Aphrodisia,
Oh, natural selection of St. Augustine and Darwin,
Oh, untranslatable God of Beethoven,
and Thou, and Thou, and Thou—
    who containest all beings, oh god of Emily Brontë,
and Thou, and Thou, and Thou—
    whose will is peace for a Dante,
and Thou, and Thou, and Thou—
Oh, Spiritual Energy of Bergson,
and Thou, the categorical imperative,
and Thou, natura naturata

and Thou, $\frac{a + b}{n}$ = x, *therefore God exists—answer!*
   of Euler, the vanquisher of Diderot,
Oh, My God,
Oh, conventional word of the poet!

As men have created Thee, Oh God, with a hundred aspects,
   showing a different face to everyone,
   so can they destroy Thee and forget.
As they have created Thee from their unnamed feelings and from
   words which in themselves mean nothing,
   so canst Thou collapse in meaningless feelings and words.
Where wouldst Thou live, if Thou wert removed from frozen hearts
   beating with anaemic blood,
where wouldst Thou stay, if, deprived of phosphorus,
   the cells of their brains closed to Thee?
I can see Thee wandering amongst the empty naves of churches and
   chapels and synagogues and mosques,
Oh, God of a hundred faces, sculpted by generations.

Then there appeared before Sebastian a form with a hundred faces
   which began to pass by, one after the other.
And among these hundred faces there were some that were as
   fathomless as the ocean,
and others that were wrinkled like the surface of a lake swept
   by the wind,
and others that were hard as diamonds.
In these faces, there were flashing eyes,
and there were others as peaceful and transparent
   as the bottom of a well.
There were lips from which a torrent of lava poured ceaselessly,
and there were others that whispered no more loudly than grass
   singing a lullaby to mosquitoes.
Some were strangers' faces, both strange and deaf,
some were distant, some very close,
some were eternal, some ephemeral,
some looked into you
and some made you look at them.

And this God said:

They did not create me so as to suffer no more,
    but because they suffer.
They did not create me so as to love,
    but because they love.
They did not create me so as to hate,
    but because they hate.
They did not create me so as to forgive,
    but to have someone to forgive them.
They couldn't contain within themselves all the passions,
    all the thirsts, all the stupidities, all the sufferings
    that are human and nothing but human,
and so they expelled, they cast out from themselves all the elements,
    all the characters of the human tragedy.
And it was from these elements that they created their gods.
I am King Lear and Desdemona, I am Iago and Lady Macbeth,
    I am Othello and Puck
        —I am at the same time bad and good, bold and cowardly,
    stupid and cunning, prodigal and miserly, material and spiritual,
    materialistic and idealistic—
I am created in the image of men,
I am Hamlet.

    It was Xenophanes who said:
    Every crime is attributed to the gods by Homer and Hesiod;
    their songs are full of everything that among mortals incurs
    censure and disapproval, every kind of shameful action: thefts,
    adulteries, mutual deceit...
    If oxen and lions had hands, if they could draw, as men can,
    they would create gods in their own image.
And if a blond angel lives in the heart of the ox, and a magnolia
    flower in that of the lion, their gods would have not only horns
    and claws, but also wings and leaves.
And if from time to time I also have an eagle's wings, a jackal's head
    and a cow's horns—like Anubis, like Isis—it's because
    men found the images of their own inner forces in the forms of

animals, each of which, like Othello, like Iago, represents a single idea, a single characteristic of human nature, and it is when they are all found within one single man that they fight each other, like the thoughts of a Hamlet, it is them that men have cast out, and it is out of them that men have created my hundred faces.
I don't know the name of the bird that Xenophanes expelled from himself in order to create a new God, whom he describes:
...there is only one God, who resembles men neither in body
nor in thought...
—but the bird of this idea also had its nest in Xenophanes himself, and—alas—this bird was also a specimen of the great zoological garden of those inner forces:
—the gods.

I am not the creator of this Universe which is made from an eighty
    digit number of protons and electrons.
I was myself created by the fragments of this Universe each of which
    is made from a billionth of billions of billions of atoms,
    fragments which are called—men.
I myself am only a creation, a work, a product, made by them.
I am only their function.

Alas, even physicists take me seriously as a creator,
    and that's why they have to reject me.
And yet, I do exist.
As the car, as the gun, as the book exist:
    it's from them that you discover men's nature.
And if you discover men's nature from their works,
    why is it their Gods that you have rejected?

Sebastian gave a start:

Yes, Thou dost exist, Thou hundred-faced God,
yes, Thou art made by men,
but art Thou also made, like their cars, of photons, electrons,
    protons and neutrons?

I am made of their thoughts. And their thoughts—
>   they are the function of those fragments of Nature,
>   each made from a billionth of billions of billions of corpuscles,
>   but are they themselves photons, electrons, protons and neutrons?
Can we measure scientifically everything that exists,
>   or is it only what we can measure that exists?'

I am a billionth of billions of billions of corpuscles,
>   and it is they who speak to their God, to their own thought:
>   *I never believed in Thee.*
>   *So Thou owest me nothing.*
>   *But the other billionths of billions of billions of corpuscles*
>   *who have gone to churches,*
>   *and chapels, and synagogues, and mosques—*
>   *they are the ones to whom Thou must give*
>   *a chunk of bread buttered with freedom,*
>   *a slice of bread covered with a radiant smile of independence,*
>   *they are the ones to whom Thou must give*
>   *a little wing of thine angel in a soup plate of the clearest*
>   *of clear soups.*

Sebastian opened wide his myopic eyes, and put on his glasses.

But he was surrounded by darkness, and it was in darkness
>   that he wrote these fragments.

IV

There are more keys on this earth, there are more keys than there are men. Everyone rattling his own bunch—and there you are: Lock them! lock them! Ladies and gentlemen! lock them! lock them! all the doors, all the packing-cases, all the cupboards, all the trunks! Lock up all the golden cages full of singing canaries!

It's the great summer shut-down.

You have no more strength, you shut your eyes too, and, with them closed, you hang on to the ski-lift, you leave down below all the packing-cases, all the cupboards and the trunks and the cages, you allow yourself to be pulled up by this enormous cable car to the peak which is waiting with its own mental reservations for somnolent skiers who have taken time off from themselves: exhausted somnambulists.

There are no somnambulists so somnolent whom the instinct of self-preservation wouldn't awaken when they're on the downward path.
But here they're on their way up, they're going up hanging on to the ski-lift, and the instinct of self-preservation is dormant, and they sleep the sleep of the exhausted, and they don't know that on the other side of the crest of the hill there is no more soft, white snow, no more swan's-down.

On Sundays Mme.B. took a parrot from her flat to her sweet-shop and put him in the window where he walked up and down amongst the jars of sweets.
People bought cakes without flour, and chocolate creams without chocolate, and the little blue parrot chanted:
'Hallo coco! hallo M'sieur B! long live the Marshal!'
and then:
'long live the young man! long live M'sieur B! hallo Marshal-coco!

But the canary is still locked up in its cage, and the Shakespeares are still in the cupboards full of camphor and naphthaline, and all the Notre-Dames are still locked in the trunks and the packing-cases that were all too heavy to be attached to the ski-lift.

'Why are you sad?' the canary—who was in his right ear—asked Sebastian. 'I don't know... I think I'm beginning to like sadness.' The canary quickly hopped out of his right ear and jumped on to the perch hanging from two very delicate little gold chains in the middle of the cage. And, moved by its enthusiasm, the perch began to swing and the little chains began to tinkle and the roundabouts started going round—in the canary's little head.

But there was no music at the fair, because it was a time of mourning.

It was in a noise without rhythm, it was in a rumbling without melody, that the swings swung, that the roundabouts went round, that the painted figures fell, hit by bullets, and that people bought tickets to see the heaviest man in the world.

The canary kept swinging higher and higher, it spread its little wings and jumped into Sebastian's left ear.

'Why are you beginning to like sadness? it asked anxiously.

'Because gaiety bores me,' replied Sebastian.

The canary made a buzzing sound with its little yellow wings and returned to its cage.

And after ten seconds, everyone came to look at Sebastian.

They jumped off the roundabouts, they brought the swings to a standstill, they stopped shooting at the painted figures.

The heaviest man in the world went to the seaside to watch the sun playing on the waves, and his ticket-seller jumped on to her stool, shouting:

'Come and see the man who likes sadness!

'Come and see the man who is bored by gaiety!

'Come and see the happiest man in the world!

'Buy your tickets, Ladies and Gentlemen, buy your tickets!

'You can beat him up, and here are some pins—five sous each—to
    stick into him.

'Do your best to make him sad, Ladies and Gentlemen!

'It'll be fun for you, and you'll make him happy,
    he said so himself, Ladies and Gentlemen!

'Ask the canary, who never lies,
    if you don't believe me!'

The canary is still shut in its cage, and all the Cervantes and all the Apollinaires are still in the cupboards full of camphor and naphthaline, and all the cloud chambers of C.T.R. Wilson[1] and all the Parthenons are still nailed up in their trunks and packing-cases.

The men looked at Sebastian, and someone said:
'It's like that because he has five fingers on his left hand.'
'But I've got five, too!' another exclaimed.
'Yes, but it's different for you!'

'Oh!' a woman shouted, 'I know! it's because he'll never see thirty-one again!'

'Go on!' another interrupted. 'I'll never see thirty-one again either, and yet...'
'Yes, but it's different for you!'

And they argued, and they already knew why it was 'like that'—so there was nothing interesting about Sebastian any more, and some people even demanded their money back from the ticket-seller. Then the heaviest man in the world had to leave the seaside and the reflections of the sun on the waves and go back to the fair, because the ticket-seller didn't want to die of starvation.

The fair-without-music went on and on, and the great summer shut-down continued. The exhausted somnambulists had no energy left; they shut their eyes, and with them closed they grabbed hold of the ski-lift, they left behind, down below, all their keys, both black and white, they left all their scores behind, and they allowed themselves to be pulled up by the immense cable car that did their thinking for them.

They were waiting for autumn and its torments to come and to remove the snow from the mountain, but the warm July night was still there, surrounding Sebastian with its greenish, star-studded darkness.

---

[1] 1869-1959, distinguished atomic physicist, celebrated for his use of the cloud chamber to study cosmic radiation.

V

I know, I know, my friend—shooting stars are only meteorites,
only particles of matter burning above us,
but at the same time they are a vibrating string—

I know, I know, my friend—a rose
is only a plant
that sings in the moist dawn,
but at the same time it is also a luminous
star.
And the sound of a violin is only oscillating air,
only a number,
I know, I know, my friend—
but for the poet it can also be a fragrant
flower,
a flower that illuminates the sky
above the stalk of darkness,
or just any flower,
after all.

You won't find it an irreparable loss,
your knowledge of this dictionary of bloodstained metaphors
that establish themselves with invincible force.

Don't be afraid, don't be afraid, my friend,
the earth will always be hard under your feet,
and this knowledge won't do any harm to your Larousses,
however complete,
however useful,
however modern.

A star that sings of the rose,
a compass rose of the howling winds
a brilliant string whose sound smells

like the milky way—
these make up only a tiny fragment of the deep forest
in which he works, the desperate poet,
the woodcutter of the planets,
the farmer of aerial vibrations,
the astronomer of plants.

There is a language of science,
interlarded with the algebra of symbols,
there is a language of senders and of receivers,
full of question marks and exclamation marks,
of dashes, brackets and inverted commas,
and there is a language of poets.

That is the Trinity of language.

I hate, I hate all the other mumblings of men who quarrel, men who persuade
one another, who proclaim, who defame, who deceive, dupe, cheat and swindle
someone or themselves,
who yell, bawl, spread rumours and who rhetoric,
who demagogue.

They think they are discovering the t r u t h
when they trample underfoot,
out of breath,
their own words, which march past us with gestures and assurance

They think they are accumulating premises
from which they can draw conclusions,
rules, principles and reasons
for everybody

These conjurors who with words stolen
half from poets and half from scientists
express their envy, their desire, their intentions,
their wishes, their will,
and who return them to us fossilized,

laying down their personal prayers
as a law
which we are obliged to obey.

They stole from the poet the discovery
that brown and black bodies fall more quickly than pale and pink ones,
They stole Galileo's formula, too,
And they juggle with these two worlds for their own ends.

They take advantage of the fact that in poetry everything is truth
that is well constructed with words from the poet's forest.
They take advantage of the fact that in science everything is truth,
that is logically constructed with words from Larousse,
words that constitute cold, objective images of reality,
and they make asphyxiating cocktails
and create syllogisms out of the poet's words,
and create imperative metaphors out of the scientist's words.

Scientists protect themselves

against the charlatans of the stars, of chemistry and of medicine,
against the astrologers, the alchemists, the bonesetters,
but even they have their hands tied.
Others commandeer their photocells,
their engines, their vitamins, their conditioned reflex formulas,
their method of thinking, which gets falsified,
but don't allow them to remake our world.

Poets don't protect themselves

In their case too, others commandeer
their sonorous words which make the surface of the skin tremble,
they commandeer their tool—the metaphor—
to use it as a crowbar
to prise open the strong-box of our good will.

Balls thrown into the air rise and fall,
sometimes according to Galileo's law
all at the same speed,
at other times according to the poet's law,
the darker ones, the duskier ones, touch the ground,
while the pale ones are still near the clouds in the azure sky,

but don't move!

They hide all the balls under a black, symbolic top hat,
they produce a magic wand,
and pull out of the parturient hat thirty-six huge alarm clocks,
one plate with a steaming omelette,
and some ribbons for the girls.

Then once again they throw up the balls
which fall according to Galileo's law,
or according to the poet's law,
into the black opera hat,
and they pull out newborn babies.

This time they have legs and a head,
they have premises and a conclusion,
yes!
but they are men's heads, and horses' legs,
and whereas centaurs belong to the domain of poets,
for them,
for administrators, directors, economists,
it is bread, commerce and schools,
houses and justice,
that it is their job to provide.

They climb up on to their trestles,
with their parturient opera hats,
and, pompously,

each says something different,
and each says it *ex cathedra*.

And it rings false, it rings false, so false!
It reverberates like a slack string!
Beat the breasts
of these jugglers with words,
these falsifiers of syllogisms,
these robbers of poetic ferries,
and you'll hear the tinny sound of a bell with a cracked soul.

Open their newspapers,
and you'll smell the putrid odour of typographic colours.

Listen to their wirelesses,
and listen! and listen!
flagellating your ears,
to that hissing sound made of a mixture of perfidious metaphors
constructed according to falsified syllogisms.

I too would like to know how to build syllogisms,
I too would like to be able to make constructions
that have the conventional form of truth,
but I don't know how many make two times two,
I'm useless when my eyes see differential & integral equations,
and instead of my brain, it's my heart that reacts
when I jump from the trampoline of this little circle around me
into the jungle of an almanac.

The world is too complicated,
the chain of cause and effect is becoming warped, and breaking,
and I am alone,
surrounded only by the music of the links of this chain,
links that vibrate like organs.

I'm not ashamed of still having blood in my veins,
of having hungers and thirsts and passions,
of having more black hairs than white ones,
of having tears that are still unshed.
The shadows of the night are filled with red flames and with mists of sobbing.
Over the surface of the moon, just as in a specimen under the microscope,
float tuberculosis bacilli
ready to fall to earth in a rain of shooting stars.
And I'm not ashamed to confess that I smile at a Colas Breugnon
reborn in 1919.

Let me go tonight into that forest
where desires and defeats,
suns and butterflies,
alphabets and smiles.
ripen on fabulous trees.
It's only that I'm giving myself a holiday,
a passive object of the phenomena of the dark hours,
as you give yourself yours
every night
while you breathe into the eiderdown of your warmed pillows,
while you dream of the steaks
that represent your hungers,
while you dream of the walking sticks and drawers
that represent your loves,
while you dream of the wage increases
that represent your struggle for the kingdom of heaven on earth.

There is a forest in which all your dreams come together
just as all your actions are brought together in an almanac.

VI

On the peel of this apple—
blood.
Dost Thou, my God, like fruit full of fighting worms?
We can put it like that—and we can put it differently:
man,
when he writes poetry,
expresses only a tiny scrap of the surface of the earth,
the one that is inside him.

Those fragments of Nature that are called physicists
formulate a 'true' reality,
and they can discover it, describe it,
always different and always the same,
by treading different paths,
by using different microscopes or scalpels.
Those fragments of Nature that are called poets
imagine their realities
growing above matter,
as flowers grow above well-nourished soil,
and they build,
with words, ideas, sounds, shapes and colours,
their different Natures
which wouldn't exist without them.

On the peel of this apple—
a song.
Dost Thou, my God, care for the noises made by men
who, thanks to the vibration of this mixture of nitrogen, oxygen et cætera,
try to climb up to the top of the apple tree,
although the apple has for a long time
been surrounded by the white solitude of a plate?

We can put it like that and we can put it differently:
man,
when he writes poetry,
expresses only a moment of eternity,
the moment that lights up inside him.

For physicists, the moment is a part of something bigger
like a second, which is only a fraction of a quarter of an hour.
But for poets, the moment is a whole world,
insoluble in the river of time,

                        picked out
                  like a sort of axiom
              upon which we can build
          the whole geometry of verse.

                                *

Round the peel of this apple—
the oracle.
Dost Thou, my God, care for the wind
anywhere else than in organ pipes?

Franciszka Themerson
London 1941

GRECIAN NIGHT

Strophe α

I am in love with her hair which is grey at dawn
I am in love with her hair which is red in the evening
Before the wind strips her
of her dress
To show me: the darkness.

Oh, summer night! warm negress,
Dusky mistress flung across the firmament,
Here, in your dark hollows,
that grey donkey, your lover, lies sleeping,
thirsting after tenderness.

And he has immortal dreams,
and he has warm visions,
they are idea-cocktails,
the magnificent sky-brothels
that he dreams in his shadowy dreams.

Oh summer night! warm Grecian night,
bathed as if in the sperm
of the milky way.
The coiled years spiral ceaselessly,
let them pass lightheartedly
like a dictation
without end.

Antistrophe α

THE GUNS HAVE FALLEN SILENT
THE PEOPLE HAVE KILLED ONE ANOTHER
PLEASE, LET TIME PASS
THROUGH THE DEPTHS OF YOUR BODY
DON'T STOP IT, DON'T STOP IT

TAKE THE GREENNESS OF NATURE IN YOUR AERIAL
                ARMS
AND LET THE PRESENT MOMENT FLEE
INTO THE DARK FORGETFULNESS OF THE DAY BEFORE YESTERDAY
        OH BITTER
        NIGHT
        OF WAR

Strophe β

Is it dried blood
that makes the earth red
like your hair, on a summer night
at the moment when you close your eyes
        joyful
     with the gaiety
       of the day
and as blue as the open Greek sea?

And as blue as the open Greek sea
between the ancient Isle of Salamis
and the village—Megalo Pefko.

Do you remember, Franciszka,
the blood-red medusa
drowned in the tepid turquoise
that our oars broke into a thousand waves?

Do you remember, my dearest
the medusa in the middle of its dreams,
that solitary Gioconda of the sea?

It was one world: its flesh
and all around—a hell
      of blue
      ephemeral
      lies.

Antistrophe β

DID SHE DREAM, LIKE THAT DONKEY
WITH THE SO-SENTIMENTAL EYELASHES
        OF THE SPIRITS OF THE DEPARTED,
            FINALLY
            HAPPY
        OR OF A GOD-GIVEN
            TRUCE
              FROM THE SCOURGE?
        OR DID SHE HAVE A BLOOD-RED
            DREAM
UNDER HER SAD EYELIDS?
DID SHE SEE, IN A BURST OF HIGH SPIRITS,
THE MEN SHE TURNED TO STONE
IN THE DAYS OF MINERVA'S SHIELD?

OH, BLUE WATER THAT DIFFUSES
THE BLOOD-RED DREAMS OF THE MEDUSAS
THAT PLUNGE INTO ITS PROFOUND DREAMS!

OH, GREEK WATER,
LET THE SECONDS PASS
LIKE THE WAVES ON YOUR SURFACE
        DON'T STOP THEM!

LET THEM CATCH THE ECHOES OF OUR FEET
AND LET THEM PASS
INTO SPACE
WITH THEM

Epode β

THE GUNS HAVE FALLEN SILENT,
THE PEOPLE HAVE KILLED ONE ANOTHER
IT'S ONLY
THE PARTHENON
THAT REMAINS
IN THE LIGHT
OF THE CELESTIAL
AZURE
IN THE SKY
THAT AZURES
THE LIGHT

THAT'S ALL WE HAVE LEFT AS REVENGE:
THE PARTHENON — THOUGHT IN WHITE STONE
HARDER
MORE PURE
THAN A PRAYER.

Epode α

The guns have fallen silent,
The people have killed one another.
Persephone! why are you sad?
After the autumn, the spring,
before the summer, the spring.
Oh, let the blood pass
through the bouquets of the florists
that are blossoming on the stones of the Acropolis.

They were selling withered flowers,
They were selling plaster saints
in their own image.

Do you remember, Franciszka,
Schubert and Schumann in miniature,
              a certain
              Pallas Athene
with an alarm clock in her belly?
            In that town
                of the eulogist
                    of Achilles.

Our florists and our flowers are dead
and our donkeys, our medusas, our days.
Oh night, let our tears pass,
expunge the blood from our love.

LA RÉVOLTE DES OREILLES
THE REVOLT OF THE EARS
BUNT USZU

'La joie vient toujours après la peine'
Apollinaire

I

Au travers de ma rivière
                coule la Seine

Au milieu de ma cité
                croît Paris

Mais la joie ne vient pas toujours après la peine

comme l'amour ne vient pas toujours après la haine

et le silence ne vient pas toujours après le cri.

2

Parce que
        il vient le temps
                où on devient **fed up**

Because the time comes
                when on en a assez

Nous nous écroulons tous
                dans une immense trappe

Bon gré—mal gré.

Vous et moi, **you and me,** ty i ja

        and Du und Ich

    too.

We all have to go down,
            far, bien loin de là

dans un pays moins doux
                que celui de nos rêves.

3

KREW
is in French: le sang,

BLOOD
c'est en anglais;

ŚPIEW
is in French: le chant

SONG
c'est en anglais;

Ah, ces frontières des mots
Ah, these frontiers of words
Ach, te granice słów.

4

Alors de nouveau la Tour
La Tour de Babel, camarades,
Et quand la gloire arriv'ra un jour
dans la Tour nous allons fêter tour à tour
a new Nationale Masquerade

    the clan—tartans
    les sabots bretons
    i łowickie kolorowe pasiaki

Couleur locale sera dieu de ce bal
after the death of the colour: khaki.

5

Je proclame la révolution

une révolte contre le mot: patrie
une révolte contre le mot: liberté
une révolte contre les mots: ayez
                              la
                              confiance

Je proclame la révolte des oreilles
Méfiance, citoyens!

Acclamons un homme d'état qui begaye.

Si notre jeu est joué avec nos corps
if our game is played with our bodies
qu'on ne nous parle pas de métaphores
qu'on ne nous parle pas: **Marble Arch freedoms**
qu'on ne nous parle pas: la liberté
we must have: bochen chleba i dom

bread—home
bon gré—mal gré.

6

      Puisque
  les mots sont à nous
  words are for us
  dla nas są słowa !

    A genoux
  les politiciens !
begayez, les orateurs, les Stentors

    we, the poets
oui, nous emmerdons
  NOUS EMMERDONS vos métaphores !

de vous on n'exige que de calculs,
messieurs les ingénieurs de notre vie
let the figures build the word: patrie
let the figures build the word: liberté
let the figures build the words: ayez
                                                      la
                                                      confiance.

A MES AMIS FRANÇAIS HABITANT L'AMERIQUE
&
TO MY AMERICAN FRIENDS LIVING IN FRANCE

The sun was shining brightly, mais le soleil était sombre,
& then le soleil brillait, but the sun went down—
always & toujours le temps—the clouds & les nuages,
always & toujours le temps—the sun & le soleil,
     But never & jamais—dans le même lieu, in the same place,
     Mais never & jamais—sur le même ciel, on the same sky.

        O mon amour, O my love,
        the source is sour, la source suave,
        & very soon
        & tout de suite
          la source—acide, & the source—sweet.

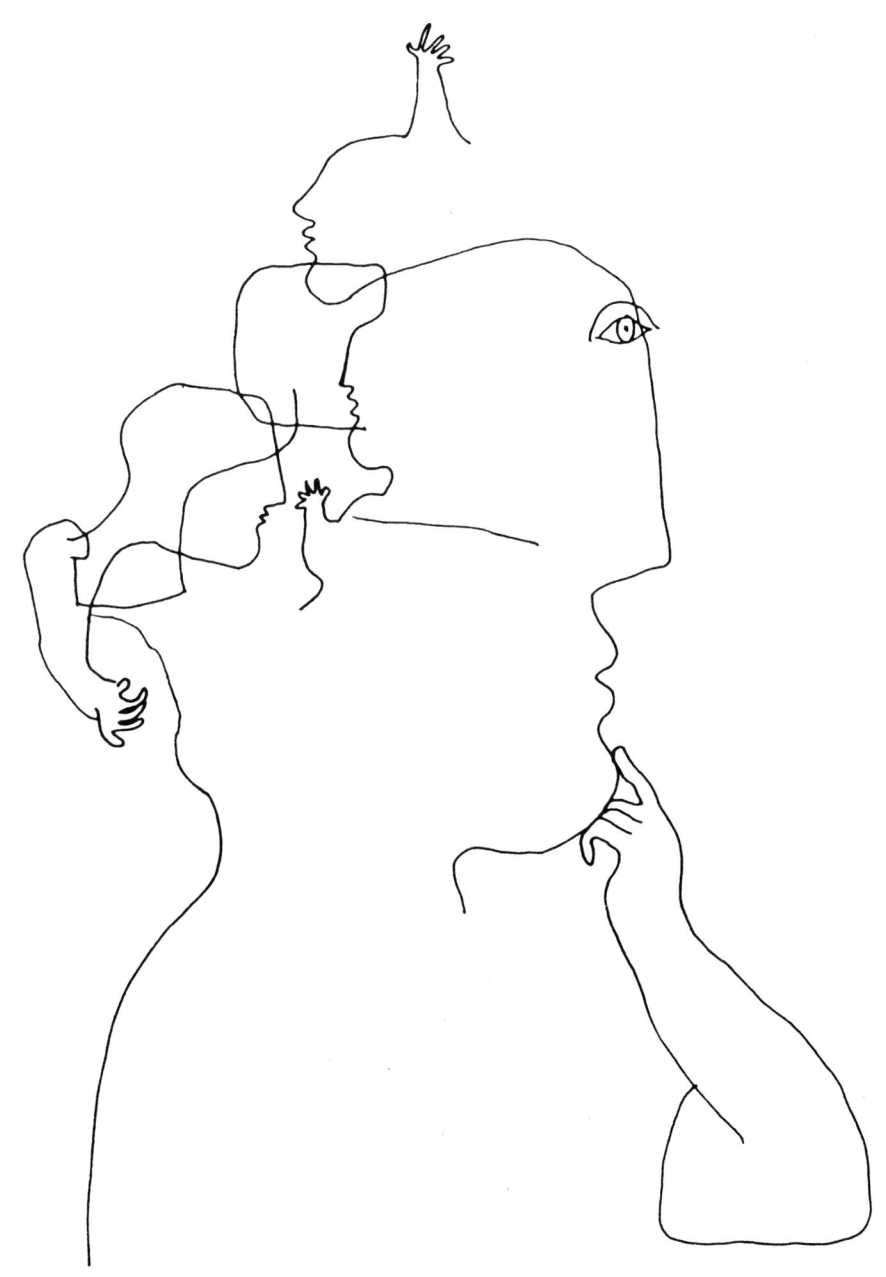

JE SÈME A TOUT VENT

Semantic poetry translation of the Quartier Latin French song sung by the woman knitting sky-blue woollen yarn

Let it continue during an extended period
that ultimate source
that primary element
that principle which pervades organic matter
and which enables persons engaged in the acquisition of knowledge
to transform food into energy
to grow
to adapt themselves to their environment
and to propagate their kind

Oh my old woman who hast the tender kindly qualities of a female parent!

Let it continue during an extended period
that state of existence in the world
that state of existence as persons engaged in a course of study at
    learned institutions!

They possess their male intromittent organs of generation
which are something stunning
> ripping
> topping
> flattening
> striking all of a heap
> astounding
> dumbfounding
> stem-breaking.

> *Et l'on s'en fout*
> *La digue digue daine*
> *Et l'on s'en fout*
> *La digue digue don!*

Let it continue during an extended period
that sum-total of functions which resist death
and which constitute the persons engaged in the acquisition of knowledge
                                of that branch of the legal profession
                    whose province it is to plead in court the cause of another

Oh my human being of female sex
oh my human being who art advancing in years
and who hath the tender kindly qualities of a mother!

Let it continue during an extended period
that vortex of chemical and molecular changes
which take place in many trillions of cells
constituting the bodies of the persons engaged in a course of studying
                the knowledge of that branch of the legal profession
                      whose province it is to plead the cause of another!

They possess their male intromittent organs of generation
made from beans of cacao plant
                          ground down
                          sweetened
                          and otherwise flavoured.

                Et l'on s'en fout
                  La digue digue daine
                Et l'on s'en fout
                  La digue digue don!

Let it continue during an extended period
that physico-chemical mechanism
of those
who apply themselves to learning the science and art
of the prevention
      treatment
  and cure of disease

Oh my human being who art still characterised by the capacity of
    bringing forth youth
oh my human being who ceasest to be capable of being fertilised and
    bearing fruit
but who hath still the tender kindly qualities of the female organism
organism from which others derive!

Let them continue during an extended period
these sum-totals of reflex actions to environment
these transformers of energy
who seek to acquire the knowledge and art of healing!

They possess their male intromittent organs of generation
made from the solid hard substance of a fir-tree trunk

> *Et l'on s'en fout*
> *La digue digue daine*
> *Et l'on s'en fout*
> *La digue digue don!*

Let it continue during an extended period
that enduring insurgent activity
growing multiplying developing
enregistering varying and evolving
that enduring insurgent activity of persons
studying the art and practice of collecting
                                preparing
                                mixing
                    and dispensing vegetable
                                      and mineral substances
                                        used for medicinal purposes

Oh my old human being
who hath the tender kindly qualities of a female parent!

Let it continue during an extended period
that dynamic equilibrium in a polyphasic system
of persons studying the science of the nature
                                preparation
                                and use of medicinal drugs!

They possess their male intromittent organs of generation
that . . .

SEMANTIC POETRY TRANSLATION OF A POLISH POPULAR SONG
the words of which,
put into English as literally as possible,
are:

HOW NICE IT IS WHEN DURING A LITLE WAR——bis——
THE UHLAN FALLS FROM HIS HORSE   ——bis——
HIS COMRADES DON'T REGRET HIM   ——bis——
THEY EVEN TRAMPLE ON HIM   ——bis——

How nice it is in that jolly good open
       conflict
      between nations
How pretty it is in that jolly smart active
       international hostility
      carried on by force of arms

When a light cavalry soldier
   armed with a weapon of offence
     & defence
    consisting of a pointed iron head
      fixed to a shaft 9
        or 10 feet in length
   used for thrusting
    & parrying

 passes through space from the level of the spine of his horse
     to the level of earth

   From the level of the spine of his horse
    to the level of earth

His partners

    participators in that open
               conflict
                between nations
companions

    associates sharing the same conditions of this active
                              international hostility
                              carried on by force of arms
            undergoing the same experiences as he does

    do not feel any grief
            sorrow
            sympathy for him

    do not regard him with desire to help
                      relieve
                      spare

They even tread upon him
        so as to crush him
                with the modified forms
                      of the toenails
                          of their horses

They even tread upon him
        so as to crush him
                with the flat strips of iron
                      shaped to fit their horses' hoofs
                      open at the back
                      placed when hot upon the under surface of the hoof
                      &
                      fastened on with nails.

SEMANTIC POETRY TRANSLATION OF THE OPENING WORDS OF A RUSSIAN BALLAD:

'HAIDA TROIKA,
THE SNOW'S DOWNY,
THE BELLS ARE RINGING...'

Haida three large powerful solid-hoofed domesticated mammals with
    long coarse flowing mane and tail
all their 3 x 4 feet in the air together
all their 3 x 4 feet in the invisible elastic gaseous substance which
    surrounds the earth
all their 3 x 4 feet having no foundation in any substance capable
    of resisting penetration by other substances
    —at one stage of each stride;
and at another stage of each stride:
all their 3 x 4 solid-hoofed feet
no more in the air
but in the multishaped crystals

```
b           b           g                                    H              L
  e           e           n                                    E              A
    l           l           i            to      to             X         N
      o   o   g                                                   A     O
              n                      to      to      to         H E X A G O N A L
        o   g   g                                                 A     O
          l   i   i                      to      to             X         N
        e       n       n                                       E              A
      b           g           g                                 H              L
```

```
                            m

                            e

       m                    t                    m
            e                              e
                 t          S         t
                       S         S
                            Y
                       S         S
                 t          S         t
            e                              e
       m                    t                    m

                            e

                            m
```

formed by the slow freezing of water vapour

Their (the crystals') texture
is like the fine soft plumage under a bird's feathers
their (the crystals') appearance
is like light fluffy substance
resembling fine soft plumage under a white bird's feathers

Hung at the necks of the three powerful solid-hoofed domesticated
    mammals
        the small
            hollow
                cup-shaped vessels of metal
                closed at the smaller upper end
                open at the larger lower end
                struck by strikers suspended inside them from the top
emit periodic compressions and decompressions of air
    periodic compressions and decompressions
    which exist independently of whether
    there is any ear to hear it
                as a clear
                    vibrating
                      resonant sound...

The T'ang Dynasty poem which is the subject of the following Semantic Poetry Translation

DRINKING UNDER THE MOON

by Li Po

The wine among the flowers,
O lonely me!
Ah moon, aloof and shining,
I drink to thee.

Beside me, see my shadow,
Rejoice we three!
Moon, why remote and distant?
Dance with my shade and me.

*

This joy shall last for ever,
Moon, hear my lay,
My shade and I can caper
Like clouds away.

And drunk we are united
(But lone by day)
Let's fix eternal trysting
In the Milky Way.

SEMANTIC POETRY TRANSLATION OF THE CHINESE POEM:
'DRINKING UNDER THE MOON' BY LI PO

*

                  The fermented
                      grape-
                      juice
        among the reproductive
                    parts
                    of
                    seed-plants

        O! I'm conscious
                of
                my state
                    of
                    being isolated
                        from
                        others!

Ah! Body attendant revolving keeping   & shining
           on   about   238,840 miles   by
           the   (mean)   reflecting the light
           Earth   aloof   radiated
                                                                                              by
                                                                                              the
                                                                                              sun

       into
       my
       mouth
     I take
       &   while expressing the hope for thy success.
       swallow
       the
       liquid

* *

    Obtain the
        visual
            impression of a
                dark
                patch formed beside me
                    by
                    my body
                      which
                        obstructs some rays of thy light!

Let   influence by feedback the object of which
us   ourselves   from   is
three   each   to stimulate
                                             the
                                           pleasure centre
                                           in
                                           our brain!

Body attendant   Why are you separated from me by 221,614 miles
    on   minimum—
    the   Why is the distance to you increasing up to 252,972
    Earth!   miles?

Make thy glides
        leaps
            revolutions
                gestures
                      & other expressions of a universal fixation for rhythmical
                                                                           movement
                          the
            keep in step with partial
                    darkness caused by the intervention
                                  of
                                  my   thy light
                                  body between
                                                      &
                                                  the surface
                                                  of the
                                                  Earth
            & with me.

* * *

```
The existence shall
    of      continue
    this    for
    emotion a                          every
            period  which is greater than assignable
            of                         quantity
            time


Body attendant   Let the    vibrations of my short lyrical song
    on                      stimulate thine external ear-drum
    the                     & be conveyed to thine internal ear-drum
    Earth!                  & thence to thine internal ear fluids
               Let them
                        cause impulses to pass up thine auditory nerve
                                    to
                                    the
                                    hearing
                                    centre
                                    in
                                    thy
                                    brain


        the
I & patch       produced by the intervention
    of darkness                 of
                                my           the surface of the Earth
                                body between
                                             &
                                             thy light


we can move
    rapidly
    like the masses   suspended   in the gases
            of          at          of
            minute      high        the
            droplets    altitudes   air
            of
            water
        away.
```

* * * *

And having the
>fermented
>>grape-juice in our stomach
>absorbing it into our cerebro-spinal fluid
>paralysing various parts of our nervous system with it
>speaking thickly
>unable to maintain equilibrium
>our vision blurred and double

we get merged with one another
>cognitively
>&
>affectively

(though separated and companionless again when the sun
>>is
>>above
>>the horizon)

Let us determine the place
>of
>our
>meeting which
>>shall
>>>continue for a period of time
>>>>greater
>>>>than
>>>>every
>>>>assignable
>>>>quantity

somewhere
between
145,000 million
>or is it
300,000 million
>stars constituting that particular 'island universe'
>>of
>>which
>>>our
>>>>solar
>>>>>system
>>>>>>is
>>>>>>>a   part.

SEMANTIC POETRY TRANSLATION OF THE PRAISE OF CREATED THINGS WHICH SAINT FRANCIS MADE WHEN THE LORD CERTIFIED HIM OF HIS KINGDOM.

Most complex
    most specialised and differentiated
    best adapted for dominating the environment more variously
                                and extensively
    having power and authority over all things
    able to do all things
    excellent in matters of conduct concerned with the difference
                                between right
                                &
                                    wrong

    virtuous
    observant of obligations
    dutiful
    conscientious
    well-behaved
    indulgent Lord

Thine be the praise
    the glory
    the honour
    & all benediction

To Thee exclusively
    only
    & to no other are they due

and no member of the highest order of mammals
    is fitted by character or quality
    to mention Thee

Be Thou glorified
    & magnified by worship
        or by recital
            esp. in song of Thy greatness
                & goodness

My Lord
    does it mean: Lord belonging to me
        or: Lord to whom I belong

Be Thou glorified
    & magnified with every one of things
            not self-existent
            but produced from nothing
                by Thee

above all
    that male and having the same parents as we
        incandescent
        approximately spherical
        heavenly body
        round which the planets of our planetary system
            rotate in elliptical orbits
    which gives the day and lightens us therewith

And it is beautiful and radiant with the great splendour
                of 114,700 tons of light pressure
                exerted on the exposed earth-surface

to Thee
    extending upwards far above any level or base
        it bears similitude

Be Thou praised
   my Owner
            of Sister Moon
            of that female and having the same parents as we
                satellite of the Earth

      & of the self-luminous celestial bodies
          intensely hot
          glowing masses
          situated at enormous distances from the solar system

       the nearest being over 4 light-years away
 in the expanse in which they move hast Thou formed them

          clear
         & precious
         & comely

Be Thou glorified
  & magnified
  my Proprietor
          of our Brother Large-Scale Movement of Air
             caused by convection effect in
             the gaseous envelope surrounding
             the Earth

             & of the composition of nitrogen
                    oxygen
                    argon
                    carbon dioxide
                    neon
                    helium
                    krypton
                    xenon
              with the addition of
                small amounts of water vapour

                                        hydrocarbons
                                        hydrogen peroxide
                                        sulphur compounds
                                    & dust particles
                            & of the masses of vapour formed in the upper atmosphere
                            & of fair and of all: bad
                                        good
                                        fine
                                        wet
                                        hot
                                        windy atmospheric conditions

by the which Thou givest to Thy creatures
                the sum total
        of environment forces
                    acting on them
                        providing their necessary food
                    and furthering their existence

Be Thou praised
    my Ruler
                of our Sister Cessation of the function of the body
                                            as an organised whole

                of our Sister Cessation of the functions of the body's
                                            many trillions of cells

            from whom no man living may escape

The divine
    supernatural anger
            vengeance
            misfortune
            misery
            ruin
            destruction will be upon those

72

                whose bodies
                            in sins incurring perdition unless repented of
                                                    and
                                                        forgiven
    ceased to function as organised wholes

                            Praise ye and bless my Lord
                                    and give Him expression of gratitude
                                                            grateful acknowledgement
                                                                        of
                                                                            obligation
                            and act as servant to Him
                                    work for Him
                                        help Him
                                        assist Him
                                    forward His interests
                                    supply Him with goods
    perform the duties of functions which He needs
                                        satisfy His wants

                                        with great meekness

                                                & lowliness of mind.

**This children's poem
served as the basis
for the Semantic Poetry translation
which follows**

*Taffy was a Welshman,
Taffy was a thief,
Taffy came to my house,
and stole a leg of beef.
I went to Taffy's house,
Taffy was not at home,
Taffy came to my house
and stole a marrow-bone.
I went to Taffy's house,
Taffy was in bed;
I took the marrow-bone,
and broke Taffy's head.*

TAFFY WAS A WELSHMAN

Taffy was a male native of Wales

Taffy was a person who practised seizing the property of another unlawfully
    and appropriated it to his own use and purpose

Taffy came to the structure of various materials
    having walls
      roof
      door
        and windows to give light and air
he came to that structure which was a dwelling for me

And there he appropriated to his own use
    one of the limbs of the dead body of an ox
    prepared and sold by a butcher

I went to the structure of various materials
    having walls
      roof
      door
        and windows to give light and air
I went to that structure which was a dwelling for Taffy

Taffy was not there

Taffy came to the structure of various materials
    having walls
      roof
      door
        and windows to give light and air
Taffy came to that structure which was a dwelling for me

And there he appropriated to his own use
        the part of the ox skeleton
        containing in its cavity
        the fat substance
        the vascular tissue
        which had formed the red bloodcorpuscles of the ox

I went to the structure of various materials
        having walls
            roof
            door
        and windows to give light and air
I went to that structure which was a dwelling for Taffy

Taffy was lying upon a piece of furniture
        consisting of a mattress
            and the wooden frame which
                supported it

I took the part of the ox skeleton
        the part containing in its cavity
        the fat substance
        the vascular tissue
        which had formed the red bloodcorpuscles of the ox

And by a sudden sharp blow
I broke open that part of Taffy's body
        situated on top of the spinal column
            which contained the great mass of nerve-cells
            the functioning of which
                is
                    mind.

THE LAY SCRIPTURE

THE LAY SCRIPTURE
or, a Draft for a Preface to a Textbook of Physics

Praise be to
>Impartiality in Thinking

Praise be to
>the Centimetre, the Gram, the Second,
>always invariant
>whether measuring
>a loaf of bread,
>the weight of an axe,
>the area of a floor,
>the height of the gallows,
>the time of peace or of war.

Reality, thou art
>hard enough a rock
>to support thoughts that flee from emotions.

God who art within me,
>allow the foot tired from wandering
>to find rest upon it.

i It is not known what was in the beginning.
Because it is not known what is: the Beginning.

ii There are those who say that the beginning is this,
there are those who say that the beginning is that;
and we do not know why we should believe
the former but not the latter,
or why we should believe
the latter but not others still
who say that there was no beginning.

   iii And as it is not known what is time without matter
by which it is measured;
and as it is not known what is matter without time
in which it is changed;
so it is not known what is universe without man
by whom it is seen;
and what is man without universe
of which he is a fragment.

   iv And it is not known
what is the meaning of the word: Genesis;
if after it must be everything
and before it nothing.

   v And man created a scripture, and he called it: Holy;
and in it he described everything that is not known.

   vi And as he saw within the beam of his eye
and within the reach of his hand
and within the moment of his life
that after **a, b** always follows;
so he called this: cause;
and he assumed that
on the scale of universes
and on the scale of atoms
and on the scale of milliards of years
and on the scale of a single vibration of an electron
that cause exists likewise & the same.

   vii So he gave a name to that Cause
and he imagined it in his own image.

   viii And he had the illusion that in this way
all that which is not known
became immediately known;
and he disregarded that which was known
and that which can be known.

ix And to those who had on their lips
that which cannot be known,
they offered their prayers
and they brought their offerings;
but they broke on the wheel
and they burned at the stake
and they drowned in the water
those who would discover and proclaim
that which can be known.

x And so it was
from the beginning of human memory
until the day of today.

xi Only the form of prayers & the form of offerings
changed with the passing centuries,
as had only changed the form of the rack.

xii One hundred years elapsed between Leonardo da Vinci
and Francis Bacon.
And it could have been ten.
And two hundred years elapsed between Francis Bacon
and Auguste Comte.
And it could have been twenty.
Yet, only four years elapsed between the conception
and the detonation of the first atom bomb.
And it could have been forty.

xiii And two hundred years elapsed between Copernicus
and Newton,
and two hundred years elapsed between Newton
and Einstein—
before the Inquisition, the Holy one & the secular one,
became resigned to the idea
that one may talk about stars & atoms,
not only by means of those words which are not known

but also by means of those words which are known;
that one may talk about stars & atoms
without employing the Hypothesis
that was already unnecessary to Pierre-Simon Laplace.

xiv And the Inquisition, the Holy one & the secular one,
ceased waging war against telescopes.
But what are telescopes & what are all instruments
but prolongations of that complicated apparatus: man?
Could we learn about the stars
if we knew only
how telescopes & spectroscopes function,
but had no idea
how an astronomer functions?

xv However, to examine man by ordinary methods
and to talk about man in words which are known
is still opposed by the Inquisition, Holy & secular.
For it says:
Heaven have we rendered
unto Copernici & Newtons & Einsteins;
but man shall we neither render
unto Darwins, unto La Mettries,
unto Pavlovs nor unto Watsons.
For that would annihilate his individuality
for that would destroy his honour
for that would crush his freedom.

xvi Do not be so jealous,
o my king, o my president, o my minister, o my priest,
for my individuality & for my honour & for my freedom.
It will do them no injury if thou throwest away
those great words which are not known.
If thou givest up a portion of thy sovereignty
to a scientific council of the earth,
which will use those words which are known
to make calculations so that there shall not be

hunger & war & illiteracy & prisons.
Take a risk,
o my king, o my president, o my minister, o my priest,
and grant the scientists that soil
which, throughout two thousand years,
the investigators of the scriptures
failed to cultivate.

xvii But in my sadness & resignation,
o my king, o my president, o my minister, o my priest,
I see that this thou wilt not do;
except thou first makest them slaves of thy mind
and prolongations of thy fingers
and instruments of thy nonsense.
It is not knowledge that directs thy acts,
but wishes, good or evil;
but desires & interests, another's or thine own;
but prejudice, great or small.

xviii But if those who should have been
engineers of temporal things
still have minds stuck in metaphysical formulae,
which can never be confirmed
and which are constructed from words
by the speculations of philosophers,
about that which is not known;
then let painters & poets & composers,
who conduct orchestras of the irrational,
let them sing to the glory of reason,
to the glory of that which is, or might be, known.

xix It will not be the first time in this world
that things come about upside down.

xx My son, born among salvos of bells
and among tolling of guns,
we shall walk together arm in arm

and sing to the glory of reason,
and shall not worship any Aristotle for ever.
And if today that which is demonstrably a truth
tomorrow is shown to be a falsehood
you will not make any tragic gestures
but with considered calm you'll delete it;
and if that which is not known
shall become that which is known
you'll insert it.
For neither those dogmas which grew from wishes,
whether good or evil;
nor those which grew from desires & interests,
whether another's or your own;
and not even those which are founded on authority
must find place, my son, in your Book.

xxi   Truth that has outlived its time
becomes: prejudice.
Truth that has been transferred
to another geographical latitude & longitude
becomes: prejudice.
How would you call, if not: prejudice
the behaviour of a man
who brings with him from Africa to London
a mosquito net,
and doesn't want to sleep without it, afraid of malaria?
How would you call
the behaviour of a modern European
who doesn't want to sit 13th at table
because two thousand years ago
Judas was 13th at the table of Jesus?
The statement that the earth is the centrum mundi
was at one time **truth**
for those who (however erroneously) **knew** it;
and at the same time **prejudice**
for those who **believed** it.

For the former,
the system described by Copernicus
was a great discovery, a revelation,
illuminating & unknotting
the complicated net of the Ptolemaic system.
For the latter,
it was a terrible revolutionary shock,
a destructive Jewish-Bolshevik invention,
as we would say in our time.
Truth that has outlived its time
becomes: prejudice.
If you call it: tradition
you will grieve me.

xxii And if they tell you that there are still moral truths,
whose time will be eternal,
say that you yourself know that better than they,
in spite of the fact that every moment you live
seems to contradict their existence.
If you go to fight
with a passer-by on the street,
your king & president & minister & priest
will come to stop you
and will enforce moral truth with their police force.
But when your king & president & minister & priest
go to fight
with kings & presidents & ministers & priests of others
there will be no moral truth to stop them
and there will be nobody
to enforce it with a police force.
And if ordinary meek men
cannot live peacefully with one another
without the rule of law,
how can you expect that those,
who through ambition & energy & forcefulness
become rulers of yours & of mine & of others,
could live peacefully with one another
without any law above them?

xxiii **Eighty sovereign states in the vineyard
and every one a wolf.**

 xxiv Sovereignty that has outlived its time
becomes: prejudice.
If you term it: tradition
you will get yourself killed.

  xxv Throw away, my son, not only the fatal-13ths,
not only the cats-crossing-the-road;
throw away also those great fantasies,
those prolegomena
of all past & present & future **meta**physics.
Learn, my son, the **ordinary** physics,
the various-branches-of-science
-dealing-with-the-material-world.
This knowledge might make you
wise & forbearing & good.

xxvi And if you become wiser & more forbearing & better
than my king & my president & my minister & my priest,
you will build on earth the republic of heaven.

```
Polska kaszkę warzyła, temu dała,temu dała,temu dała, a temu łebek urwała, O!
olska  aszkę  arzyła,  emu  ała, emu  ała, emu  ała,     emu  ebek  rwała, O!
 lska   szkę   rzyła,   mu   ła,  mu   ła,  mu   ła,      mu  bek   wała, O!
  ska    zkę    zyła,    u    a,   u    a,   u    a,       u   ek    ała, O!
   ka     kę     yła,                                       k         ła, O!
    a      ę      ła,                                                   a, O!
                                                                         O!
    a      ę      ła,                                                   a, O!
   ka     kę     yła,                                       k         ła, O!
  ska    zkę    zyła,    u    a,   u    a,   u    a,       u   ek    ała, O!
 lska  aszkę   rzyła,   mu   ła,  mu   ła,  mu   ła,      mu  bek   wała, O!
olska  aszkę  arzyła,  emu  ała, emu  ała, emu  ała,     emu  ebek  rwała, O!
Polska kaszkę warzyła, temu dała,temu dała,temu dała, a temu łebek urwała, O!
Polsk  kaszk  warzył, tem dał ,tem dał ,tem dał , a tem łebe  urwał , O!
Pols   kasz   warzy , te  da  ,te  da  ,te  da  , a te  łeb   urwa  , O!
Pol    kas    warz  , t   d   ,t   d   ,t   d   , a t   łe    urw   , O!
Po     ka     war   ,                            , a     ł     ur    , O!
P      k      wa    ,                            , a           u     , O!
              w     ,                            , a                   O!
P      k      wa    ,                            , a           u     , O!
Po     ka     war   ,                            , a     ł     ur    , O!
Pol    kas    warz  , t   d   ,t   d   ,t   d   , a t   łe    urw   , O!
Pols   kasz   warzy , te  da  ,te  da  ,te  da  , a te  łeb   urwa  , O!
Polsk  kaszk  warzył, tem dał ,tem dał ,tem dał , a tem łebe  urwał , O!
Polska kaszkę warzyła, temu dała,temu dała,temu dała, a temu łebek urwała, O!
Polska kaszkę warzyła, temu dała,temu dała,temu dała, a temu łebek urwała, O!
Polsk  kaszk  warzy , temu dała,temu dała,temu dała, a temu łebek urwał , O!
Pols   kasz   warz  , temu dał ,tem dał ,tem dał , a tem łebe  urwa  , O!
Pol    kas    war   , tem dał ,tem dał ,tem dał , a tem łeb   urw   , O!
Po     ka     wa    , te  da  ,te  da  ,te  da  , a te  łe    ur    , O!
P      k      w     , t   d   ,t   d   ,t   d   , a t   ł     u     , O!
Po     ka     wa    , te  da  ,te  da  ,te  da  , a te  łe    ur    , O!
Pol    kas    war   , tem dał ,tem dał ,tem dał , a tem łeb   urw   , O!
Pols   kasz   warz  , temu dała,temu dała,temu dała, a temu łebe  urwa  , O!
Polsk  kaszk  warzy , temu dała,temu dała,temu dała, a temu łebek urwał , O!
Polska kaszkę warzyła, temu dała,temu dała,temu dała, a temu łebek urwała, O!
Polska kaszkę warzyła, temu dała,temu dała,temu dała, a temu łebek urwała, O!
Polska kaszkę  arzyła, temu dała,temu dała,temu dała, a temu łebek rwała, O!
olska  aszkę   rzyła, temu dała,temu dała,temu dała, a temu łebek wała, O!
 lska   szkę    zyła, temu dała,temu dała,temu dała, a temu ebek  wała, O!
  ska    zkę     yła,  emu  ała, emu  ała, emu  ała, a  emu  bek   ała, O!
   ka     kę      ła,   mu   ła,  mu   ła,  mu   ła, a   mu   ek    ła, O!
    a      ę       a,    u    a,   u    a,   u    a, a    u     k    a, O!
```

St. Themerson, 1946.

Poland cooked a pot of porridge,

She gave some to this one, and this one, and this one, and this one

and she wrung the neck of this one

(Original Nursery Rhyme "A little hen cooked a pot of porridge &c

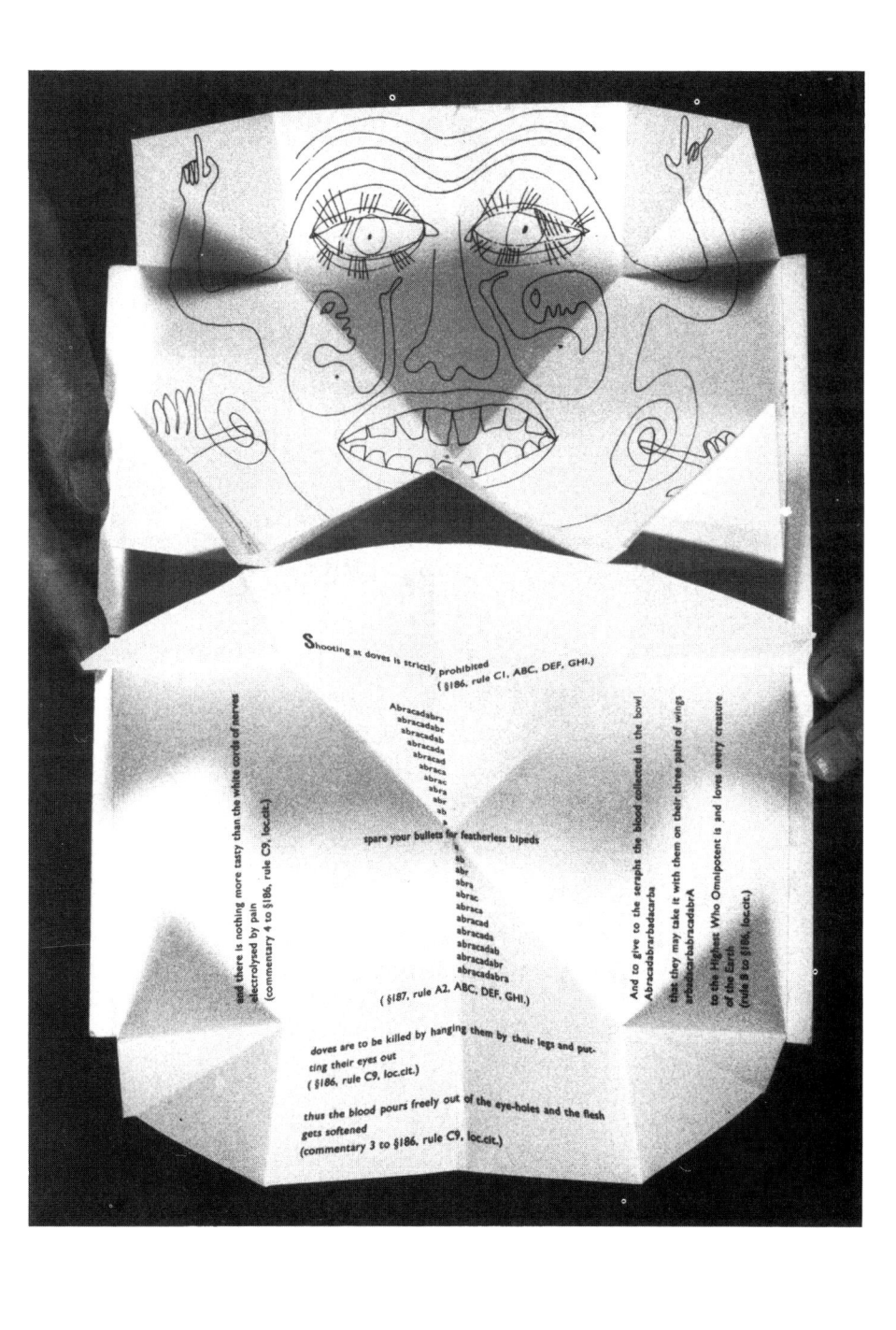

Shooting at doves is strictly prohibited
(§186, rule C1, ABC, DEF, GHI.)

Abracadabra
abracadabr
abracadab
abracada
abracad
abraca
abrac
abra
abr
ab
a

spare your bullets for featherless bipeds

a
ab
abr
abra
abrac
abraca
abracad
abracada
abracadab
abracadabr
abracadabra

(§187, rule A2, ABC, DEF, GHI.)

and there is nothing more tasty than the white cords of nerves electrolysed by pain
(commentary 4 to §186, rule C9, loc.cit.)

And to give to the seraphs the blood collected in the bowl
Abracadabrabracadabracarba
that they may take it with them on their three pairs of wings
arbacarbabracadabrA
to the Highest Who Omnipotent is and loves every creature of the Earth.
(rule 9 to §186, loc.cit.)

doves are to be killed by hanging them by their legs and putting their eyes out
(§186, rule C9, loc.cit.)

thus the blood pours freely out of the eye-holes and the flesh gets softened
(commentary 3 to §186, rule C9, loc.cit.)

ABRACADABRA

shooting at doves is strictly prohibited
§ 186, rule C1, ABC, DEF, GHI
Abracadabra
  abracadabr
    abracadab
      abracada
        abracad
          abraca
            abrac
              abra
                abr
                  ab
                    a

spare your bullets for featherless bipeds
a
ab
abr
abra
abrac
abraca
abracad
abracada
abracadab
abracadabr
abracadabrA
§ 187, rule A2, ABC, DEF, GHI

Doves are to be killed by hanging them by their legs
                        and putting their eyes out
§ 186, rule C9, loc.cit.

thus the blood pours freely out of the eye-holes
and the flesh gets softened
commentary 3 to § 186, rule C9, loc.cit.

and there is nothing more tasty than the white cords of nerves
electrolysed by pain
commentary 4 to § 186, rule C9, loc.cit.

and to give to the seraphs
the blood collected in the bowl
abracadabrArbadacarba

that they may take it with them
on their three pairs of wings
arbadacarbAbracadabra

to the Highest Who
Omnipotent is and loves
every creature of the Earth
rule 8 to § 186, loc.cit.

ELEGY IN A LONDON BUS

Having just had his tongue examined (1951) by an old£British, and his ear by a young$American civil servant, the Author in a reflective and melancholy mood gives expression to the thoughts called up in his mind by the sight of a lonely ladybird found in the upper part of a London bus No 6.

Squeezed ¼ between the iron curtain and the Atlantic wall ½ the red ladybird ½ red double-decker three halfpenny fare ¼ of my and of your freedom ¾
between Selfridge's and Bumpus's ½ from Marble Arch to Oxford Circus ½ above the hatless heads of the harassed rush-hour women ¾

There are no plant-lice there and no eggs of insects ¼ upon which it could feed ½ there is no force there ¼ but symbols of force ½ there is no agency ¼ but symbols of agencies ¼ at work in the world ¼ between Selfridge's and Bumpus's ¼ from Marble Arch to Oxford Circus. Not physical processes there ¼ but symbols of physical processes ½ not causes and effects ¼ but symbols of causes and effects ¼ of the rush hour ½ between Selfridge's and Bumpus's. There are no laws there ¼ but man-made symbols of laws ¾ there are no miracles ¼ but man-made symbols of miracles ½ from Marble Arch to Oxford Circus. There is no Nature between Selfridge's and Bumpus's.

And we need Nature more than we need mass on Sunday morning. Lost ¼ among symbols of tweed and serge suits ½ of dropped and pronounced hs ½ of iron ½ stone ½ calculus ½ we need green leaves more than we need Ascensions and Assumptions. Yet the lamppost is the tree of our forest.

There is no room for me in that three-halfpenny fare ½ from Marble Arch ¼ to ¼ to Oxford Circus ¾ the red double-decker of my freedom ½ the red ladybird ¼ look! ¼ is crushed under the heels of the harassed women ½ rushing ¼ during that hour.

(note: ¼, ½, ¾, ., indicate relative duration of silence.)

A SONG OF A FLEA

        I've met a man
              poor man
                      poor man
                      who has never seen anything
And what am I to do with him
                  poor man
            poor man

I may bite his nose. It won't make him see anything
He'll ask his doctor to give him some medicine.

I may bite his buttocks. He will still see nothing
He'll ask his wife to scratch under his clothing.

I may let him catch me, and kill me, but he still
Won't see that Jesus Christ was so very close to him.

I am waiting...

I am waiting for my Lord the Dentist
In the Dentist's empty waiting room
Why do they always send me to the Dentist
If what pains me is my heart and not the calcareous structures
occupying the alveolar processes of the upper and lower jaw,
and serving to tear, cut and grind my food?

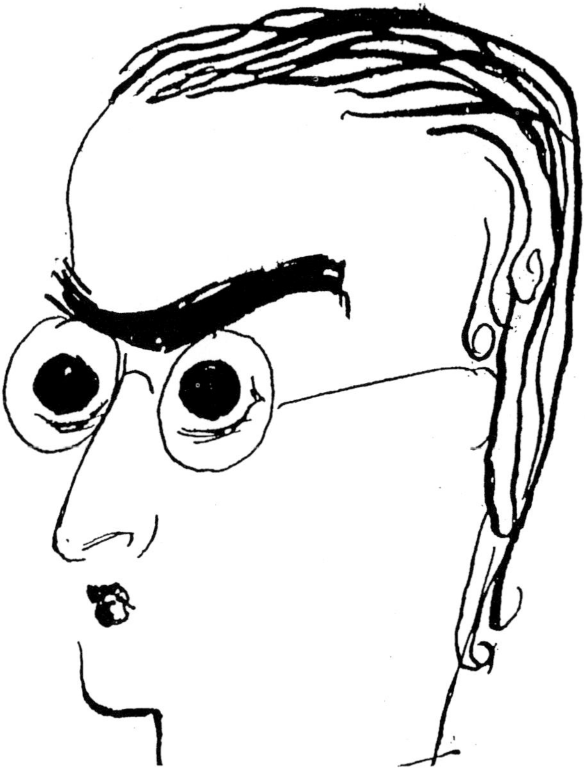

SEMANTIC SONATA

1st MOVEMENT
Exposition
Semantic development
Recapitulation and Coda

2nd MOVEMENT
Theme and Three Variations

3rd MOVEMENT
Litany in ZED (in place of Scherzo)

4th MOVEMENT
Exposition
Development (verboidal and semantic)
Reminiscence of the Litany
Recapitulation
Coda

SEMANTIC SONATA

1st
MOVEMENT
Exposition

1st phrase

> I've got a white rag to gag a demagogue with
> a white rag of logic I've got and am holding it in my hand
> but he's so tall, O my God, and his mouth is so far from the ground
>
> I climb up and climb and climb up and up
> have been climbing
> since the first day of Genesis
>
> yet the nail of his ogreish toe
> still keeps high above my outstretched fingers

2nd phrase

>> Simple words build gothic cathedrals
>> words like: earth
>> words like: knife
>> words like: wood
>>
>> Simple syntax builds dodecahedrons
>> syntax like: I was there
>> syntax like: You give it to him
>> syntax like: Prisoner at the bar, you have been convicted
>>   on very clear evidence.
>>
>> Simple words upon my writing desk
>> Simple syntax—behaviour of my muscles

      And
        nevertheless
Here I am, pretending to be what I'm not
Pretending to hear, and—deaf,
pretending to sing, and—voiceless,
pretending to love, and—ashes.

God gave me human shape, and said: Pretend!
God always gives some shapes to his voids and says: Pretend! And
the voids do pretend, and grow old, and become
what they were not,
what they didn't want to be.

Semantic development (1)

  I am in possession of a tatter of irregular shape
       torn from a larger piece
      and
      having the colour of unstained snow
and suitable for the purpose of filling with it the mouth
        of one
       who stirs up by oratory and
         leads or attempts to lead
        the people
       who appeals to popular emotion,
         rather than to reason.
But he is so above the average in stature
      —o somebody-else's Assumption
       o somebody-else's most august reality!—
and it's a long way the way to his larynx.

I pull and propel myself upwards
 using my hands and
     feet

  I grow up, along him,
   holding by means of my tendrils,
  I mount and rise in the world,
   attain an important position by dint of
     effort,
  I get higher up, raise myself, ascend,
    have
  been exerting
  considerable energy to this end

since the day when de Lawd
    He done go work hard
    for make dis ting dey call um Earth,
since the days when de Lawd
    He work
    an' He done make all ting—
    every'ting He go put for Earth
      plenty beef,
      plenty cassava
      plenty banana,
      plenty yam,
      plenty guinea corn,
      plenty mango,
      —everyt'ing—
since the day de Lawd take small piece Earth
  an' He go breathe—
  an' man day

Yet the layer of horny substance
  covering and growing beyond the
  upper surface of the tip
    of the digit
    of his foot
still keeps high above the muscles of my fingers
    extended fully
     forcibly

Semantic development (2)

    The free from complexity
                      or
           intricacy,
         direct,
          clear
arrangement of the ultimate units of speech in sentences
              builds the what-you-call Useless
                      useless vertical lines
                      large unobstructed interiors
                      immense shells of vaulting
                            covering nave
                                and
                                high side aisles
                      in one span,
                the sharply tapering summits in the
                    non-utilitarian achievements of
                    the class of human beings,
                the highest points in the not-the-
                    greatest-happiness-of-the-greatest-
                    numbery gains of the me-and-you-and-others,

an arrangement like: This portion of space-time is: I,
                      that portion of space-time is: there
                        this & that have a common part
an arrangement like: you transfer
                    this something
                    good or bad
              material or non-material
       whether for nothing or in exchange for something else
                from your own possession
                        control
                  to that of his

an arrangement like: Person under arrest and in custody,
                    charged with a crime
                            or
                            offence
                who are standing now
                    at the railing in this court of law
                    at the railing which separates from the
                            rest of the hall
                            the part
                            where we, judges, sit,
                            where you, persons under arrest
                                    and in custody,
                                    charged with a crime
                                    or offence, who are
                                    standing now at the
                                    railing in this court
                                    of law, at the railing
                                    which separates from
                                    the rest of the hall
                                    the part
                                    where we,
                                            judges,
                                            sit,
                                    where you,
                                        persons
                                                under
                                                arrest
                                                and
                                                    in
                                        custody . . . . . .

2nd
MOVEMENT

Theme

    What is ceiling for my neighbour downstairs
        is floor for me
  How can we ever find one another
        if
        unwilling
          to replace words by terms
        and to call it: Horizontal structure of wood or other material
                dividing storeys of a building.

1st
Variation

      Sugar is soluble in water;
      Is one molecule of sugar soluble in a ton of water ?

      Sugar is soluble in water;
      Is one molecule of sugar soluble in a molecule of water ?

      Sugar is soluble in water;
      Is one ton of sugar soluble in a molecule of water ?

      Sugar is soluble in water;
      Is one molecule of sugar—sugar ?

2nd Variation

>What's a molecule for my neighbour downstairs
>>is sweet for me
>
>How can we ever find one another?
>What's a ton for my neighbour above
>>is white for me
>
>How can we ever meet?

3rd Variation

>Green pigments build the white crystalline substance
>green pigments contained in the leaves of green plants;
>Is one second of tomorrow—tomorrow?

3rd
MOVEMENT

Litany in ZED
(in place of Scherzo)

        It's not for me to say so
        It's not for you to say so
        It's not for him to say so

            Zephyr
            Zoroaster
            Zorobabel

        It's not for me to change you
        It's not for you to change him
        It's not for him to change me

            Zealand
            Zingaro
            Zuyder Zee

        It's I who have to change myself
        It's you who have to change yourself
        It's he who has to change himself

            Zwieback
            Zurbaran
            Zwingle

        It's I whom I have to change
        It's you whom you have to change
        It's he whom he has to change

            Zambo
            Zero
            Zoo

4th
MOVEMENT

Exposition
1st phrase

        Yesterday you were right
                The happiness of the greatest number
    But you don't know that during the nightmare
                hours
    The natural laws have changed. And today
    what was your truth is no more ours than
                The gostak distims the doshes.

    And if the gostak distims the doshes
            then the doshes are distimmed by the gostak
            and at least one distimmer of doshes is a gostak.

    And if, moreoever, the doshes are galloons
            then at least some galloons
            are distimmed by the gostak.

2nd phrase

I must eat bread to be able to read a book;
So they come in through the crevices in my attic and sermonize: 'See?
$$\text{Bread is the thing!}$$
You shouldn't read the book
unless it is about bread'.

        he
        hedo
        hedonis

I must drink soup to be able to paint a picture;
So they come in through the crevices in my attic and hiss: 'See? Soup
$$\text{is the thing!}$$
What you should paint is a soup-plate
                with the happiness of the greatest number'.
        phee
        philo
        philoso

Development
(verboid and semantic)
(I)

       Yesterday you were right

           he
           hedo
           hedonis

       The gostakness of the greatest number

           phee
           philo
           philoso

       But during the night hours

           he
           hedo
           hedophers

the new class of demagogues in the crevices of my attic grew up

           phee
           philo
           philonis

and what was the young man's creed became the grown-up's gostak.

        Uni versal istic he
And if the gostak distims the doshes
        doni stikfi philo so
then the doshes are distimmed by the gostak
        phersu niver salis tik
and at least one distimmer of doshes is a gostak
        hedo nistic fifi lo

        Sophers uni versal is
And if, moreover, the doshes are galloons
        tikhe doni stikfi fi
then at least some galloons
        loso phersu niver sal
are distimmed by the gostak
        istic hedo nistic fi

        Philo sophers uni ver
        salis tikhe doni stic
        fifi loso phersu ni
        versa listic hedo nis

        Tikfi philo sophers u
        niver salis tikhe doh
        nistik fifi loso phers
        uni versa listic he

**Development
(verboid and semantic)
(2)**

        Flour and water
        mixed with yeast
        and baked
        must enter the functional whole of my body
           and repair
           and build up protoplasm
                whose activity in my brain is: thought

Simple things build up protoplasm
    things like: flour
    things like: water
    things like: yeast

Simple words buildagothicca-thedral
    words like: flour
    words like: water
    words like: yeast

    Yet its tower
    is the thought
    of its buttresses.

**Reminiscence
of the Litany**

                  I am a minority of one
                  You are a minority of one
                  He is a minority of one
                  Is one molecule of love—love?

Recapitulation

                  Words about words
                  are about words
                  but words
                  are about the rest of the world.

                  And even words about words about words
                  will not reach you
                  without that part of the world
                  which isn't words.

Coda

I've let the cat out of yesterday
                yesterday's picture of the world
                yesterday's picture of
of the world built of words
                yesterday's picture
picture built of words like: gostakness
                doshes
                galloons
But I don't see tomorrow
but I can't see tomorrow's picture of the world
        tomorrow's picture
        tomorrow...

A void with a white rag to gag another void with
I am an empty envelope. You receive it
and search for the sender's address, and look at the post-office stamp
and x-ray, and y-ray, and z-ray it
and fill me, the void, with your xyz mysteries—

I am an empty exoskeleton. Life receives it
and kicks it, and strokes it, and fills it with viscera
and the viscera fill the void, and grow old, and become
what they were not,
what they didn't want to be.

A white endocrine rage I've got and am holding it in my larynx
But I don't see tomorrow
        tomorrow's picture of the world
        tomorrow's picture
        tomorrow

What is it that he wants...

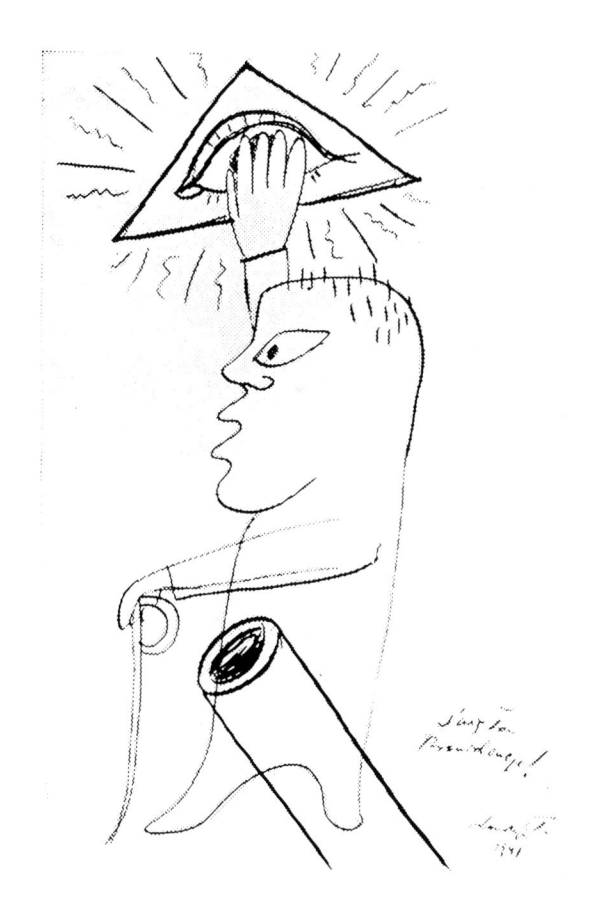

What is it that he wants to be hidden
from the Eye of Providence
from the eye that isn't part of a head
part of a head that would stick on a neck
on a neck that would grow from a trunk
from a trunk that would have two long arms
with which to avenge us.

CASTOR & POLLUX

And so they went to the house of Bogalawd.
'I wish you were dead,' said Bogalawd.
Pollux turned to Castor and asked:
'Ought we not to cut his head off?'
Castor directed a penetrating, searching look at Bogalawd's head for the purpose of examining it thoroughly and forming a judgment concerning it.
'Not worth it,' he said. 'Such a poor head. No more than two poor eyes, and one poor nose, and one poor mouth!'
'I wish you were dead,' repeated Bogalawd.
'Why?' asked Pollux.
'You don't know what life is like. I mean here, in my house, all around; and below, in the basement.'
'Many people?' asked Castor.
'Oh,' answered Bogalawd, 'Many too many. They live as in hell.'
'Cannot one help them?' asked Pollux.
'No,' said Bogalawd. 'Impossible. They are unhappy.'
'Well?' asked Castor.
'Every single method applied in order to ease them will itself add to their unhappiness.'
''tsapity,' said Pollux.
Castor sighed and said:
'May we not stay here, in the hall, until the morning twilight, when the sky will be illuminated by the reflection of the rays of the rising sun on the clouds of dust, &c., suspended in the atmosphere, before it will rise above the horizon. May we not wait here until the dawn is clear bright yellow, or for even shorter time, until it is gold, or only until it is orange, or at least until it is deep red. Could you not bring us a bed here?'
'I certainly could,' said Bogalawd, 'but there are not many beds down there. So they'll be even more unhappy if I take one away.'
'Well,' said Castor, 'and could you not bring us a glass of water, for we are craving for something to drink.'
'I certainly could,' said Bogalawd, 'but there are many there who experience thirst, who have a need of liquid in their systems; so if I take some water from them it will add to their unhappiness.'
'Well,' said Castor, 'there is nothing for us to do here but to say good-bye and go straight away.'

'You certainly can say good-bye and go straight away,' said Bogalawd, 'but the floor between the door and that part upon which you are now standing is rotten, and it screams when one puts one's foot upon it. And, below, there live women who have headaches, cerebrotonic men who write poetry, and nervous children who fear screech-owls. And the screeching produced by the rotten timber when you are going from here to the door will add to their unhappiness.'

'Then what can we do?' said Castor.

'Nothing!' said Bogalawd. 'I said I wished you were dead.'

'But if we die here, where we stand,' said Pollux, 'and what we are built of remains here, it will decompose and then there will be a smell which will add to their unhappiness.'

'Oh, no!' said Bogalawd. 'They like the smell of dead bodies decomposed by *natural* processes through exposure to air, moisture &c. The natural full-smelling decomposition of organic matter—that's what they like most of all; it will not add to their unhappiness.'

'If that is so, pray kill us,' said Castor.

'If that is so, pray kill us,' said Pollux

But Bogalawd said:

'I don't like to kill. If you want to be killed, you can yourselves kill yourselves.'

'Is it feasible?' asked Castor.

'It isn't' said Pollux. 'If *A* is doing something, and *B* comments on what *A* is doing, *B*'s action is of a higher order than *A*'s action. If *B* is killing *A*, killing is of a higher order than living. And if I am killing myself, *I* belong to a higher order than *myself*. Well, *I* can kill *myself*, but who is going to kill *I*? And who is going to kill him who will kill *I*? And who is going to kill him who will kill him who will kill *I*? And who is going to kill him who will kill him who will kill him who...'

'Nonsense,' said Bogalawd. 'Modern philosophy is nonsense. You forget that you are double, and that Castor may kill Pollux and Pollux may kill Castor. I mean: at the same moment.'

'Do you think so?' said Castor.

'Let us try,' said Pollux.

So Pollux placed the point of his sword upon the breast of Castor, and Castor placed the point of his sword upon the breast of Pollux, and they thrust them simultaneously through their respective bodies.

And that is the true story about the end of the two brothers of Helen, the children of Leda. Amen.

ON THE RISE AND FALL OF THE ONLY CHRISTIAN CHURCH FOUNDED BY A WOMAN

I liked the wedding-cake whiteness of this female Vatican
Whose Little Mother Kozłowska was the Pope, the Hippopotamus,
    and the Rock.
Perhaps I wanted to be the little boy whom one could always see
    there, playing in the Cloister garden,
And who was either her son, or a bastard whom her church adopted.

And when she died (I remember watching her waxen body swelling
    in a glass coffin;
she wouldn't allow a doctor to drain her diseased bladder),
The Cloister joined the Monastery,
And Vespers—they said—were danced to the music played by
    naked mandolinists.

The little boy, if alive, must be an old man now,
And I wonder, Why it is always plucking instruments
That accompany the Falls of great and small empires?
Lyres, balalaikas, guitars.

The king of Sweden...

The king of Sweden who conquered Poland in the XVIIth century
said to the queen of England who conquered India in the XIXth century
'You know, Madam, I saw a crab that was red in the sea
and green in the saucepan.
Isn't it odd. Isn't it extraordinary?'

SOME YEARS AFTER HIS DEATH

Djugashvili, Djugashvili, where have you been?
I've been to Tiflis, to visit my Theological Seminary.

Djugashvili, Djugashvili, why did you go there?
I went there because
I'd nowhere else to go.

Djugashvili, Djugashvili, what did you see there?
Our Lord, Jesus Christ, touched up by Goya.

Djugashvili, Djugashvili, what did He say?
He said:
Sweeter one who recants
Than 10 million dead convicts.

That little thing...

That little thing, miscalled by the Church:
                                      'immortal'
Is killable.
Not only self-destructible
but killable.
Either before the death of our body
or at the same time
or after.

HOLY VIRGIN

Who created Thee who
    created Thee who created
        Thee who created Thee
            who created Thee—Holy Virgin?

Who invented Thee who
    invented Thee who invented
        Thee who invented Thee
            who invented Thee—Holy Virgin?

Kind of men
    of men of what kind
        of what kind of men
            what kind of men were they
(Because they were not women).

Would I like them?
Would I like to meet them?
Would I like to have them to tea?

PILATE

He didn't wash his hands
He washed his brain,

Fascists and some anti-fascists...

Fascists
and some anti-fascists
have one thing in common.
They think that the difference
between a member of one nation
and another
is bigger than the difference between
a male & a female, an old man & a young man,
a pyknic and an asthmatic,
and that the difference between one country
& another is bigger than the difference between
an island & a continent, between
mountains & steppes, between the forests of
pines & the canyons of skyscrapers.

There are there...

There are there there are here there are
fascists
and anti-fascists
and there are anti-anti-fascists.
And anti-anti-fascists
are both
anti-fascists & anti anti-fascists.

It is necessary but not enough to counterbalance
fascists with anti-fascists.
You need anti-fascists-anti-anti-fascists
to have something positive to live for.

P.M.

Here they are, Sir, straight from the lab,
Two slices of the two hearts you wanted to see.
I have no doubt that you will be able to establish
Which one is young, which is old,
Which is worn out, which is fresh,
Which belonged to a woman, which belonged to a man;
Perhaps, even, what ate them,
Perhaps, even, who fed them,
Perhaps, even, which one killed which.

But no electron-microscope will tell you,
No chromatography will ever distinguish,
Which heart belonged to the man marked 'a German',
And which to the man marked 'a Jew'.

LOVE OF NATIONALS

I have studied the subject, I know all the reasons
Why I should love a Pole more than any other national.
But I do not, I'm sorry, I don't know why, but I do not.

It is strange...

It is strange that such a great nation as the English, hasn't got
its own language, but must share it with the Welsh, the Scots, the
Irish, with the Americans, Canadians, Australians, with New Zealanders
and South Africans, with the Indians, the Negroes and with myself.

Dost thou not know...

Dost thou not know, my son, with how little wisdom the world is governed?[1] There are but two families in the world, as my grandmother used to say, the Haves and the Havenots.[2] And they have learnt nothing, and forgotten nothing.[3] They can do no otherwise.[4] I sit on a man's back, choking him and making him carry me, and yet assure myself and others that I am very sorry for him and wish to ease his lot by all possible means—except by getting off his back.[5] Men use *thought* only to justify their wrongdoings, and *speech* only to conceal their thoughts.[6] O! liberty! O! liberty! what crimes are committed in thy name![7] One should never put on one's best trousers to go out to battle for freedom and truth.[8] Politics is not an exact science.[9] Remember:[10] Whoever could make *two* ears of corn or *two* blades of grass to grow upon a spot of ground where only *one* grew before, would deserve *better* of mankind, and do *more* essential service to his country than the whole race of politicians put together.[11]

1 Count Oxenstjerna
2 Cervantes
3 Talleyrand
4 Martin Luther
5 Tolstoy
6 Voltaire
7 Mme Roland
8 Ibsen
9 Bismarck
10 Charles I
11 Swift

I don't read poetry...

I don't read poetry
(unless I have to)
And I look with some suspicion
at those who do.

Because poems don't need to be read
though they have to be written.
Such is the law of nature:
Caterpillars must change into butterflies
But that does not mean
that butterflies have to be eaten.

Yes,
there may be nothing wrong with a kingdom or a republic
Where nobody reads poetry,
But there's definitely something wrong with the one
where nobody writes it.

Because
it is wrong for caterpillars not to change into butterflies.

And here is the end of the story.
I think it is quite sufficient
just to know that they exist
(I mean: butterflies)
And this is why I look with great suspicion
at those who
eat them.

I admire poets...

I admire poets who can put words into such a form
That you can almost take it in your fingers
And place it on a lady's head, like a tiara,
Or on an art historian's desk, like a paperweight.

Yes, I admire many things that I don't like.

I can't read your poetry...

I can't read your poetry,
Life seems so much richer without it.
Just like death seems so much richer
without the beautiful & elaborate
wreath hung above a grave.

FREE-CASSEE

ON THE POETRY OF MONOPLANES AND BATHYSPHERES

Neither T. S. Eliot
is as winged as a Blériot
Nor Ezra Pound
très profound.

TO HEINRICH HEINE

You sentimental bastard, did you reallei
lorelei Lorelei in her blonderei mahlerei?
Or was it all a hoax, a reversed Anna Livia
to cover vulgar truth with drôles de trivia?

A REGRETTO

Jarry's Shakespearian horror comic
is sickly weak in times atomic:

Ubu was grim enough a Roi
pour épater les bourgeois;

Not grim enough today, alas!
pour épater la populace.

GOYA'S PICTURES

'What cruelty!'   1816
'Because she was sensitive'   1820
'He loved a she-ass'   1826
'Because her parents were Jewish'.

We cannot comprehend...

We cannot comprehend
the world without assuming
that there is something
incomprehensible in it.

If I don't despair...

If I don't despair at the thought that
I shall never know why the world is what it is,
it is not that I'm very wise, but
that I'm not very silly.

It would have been comic...

It would have been comic
To call a horror strip a horror comic
If an example
Had not been given by Honoré Balzac and Dante.

TO ENCOURAGE THE APPLICATION OF MATHEMATICAL METHODS TO HISTORICAL ANALYSIS

Each offers a concrete demonstration
of the advantages and limitations of this new approach

1. (visual)

Enjoy your bath soon all the waters of the world will harden into sharp cold crystals of hate sparkling with millions of enchanting rainbows whose nature it is to be in as many positions in space as there are eyes in all the heads bobbing up and down on the surface

2. (vocal)

Enjoy your bath   Soon
all the waters of the world will harden
into sharp cold crystals of hate
sparkling with millions of enchanting rainbows
whose nature it is
to be in as many positions in space
as there are eyes in all the heads
bobbing up and down on the surface

NOBODY KNOWS

There are two ways
of seeing the ways of seeing the world:
One is one way, and the other is another.

And nobody knows:—
'Is there anywhere one way
of seeing the two?'

A MILLION WAYS

Hunger
teaches you wisdom.
But it is only one kind of wisdom.
A full stomach teaches you another.

O, God, how silly, very silly:
A hundred ways of being wise
and none can cut across the maze
of a million ways of being stupid.

The worst has already happened...

The worst has already happened
Though not to us
Well, then, let's forget about it
History doesn't repeat itself
It's you who repeat it
hoping the rain
will turn to flood not here
but somewhere else
again.

When I reflect on Nature's cruelty...

When I reflect on Nature's cruelty
am I a part of her? Because, if so,
then moral judgments are a natural thing.
And, if they aren't, then how can I, who hold them,
      a part of Nature be?

Yet, if you say that I'm a part of Nature
      but my judgement isn't,
You say that she spawns something that isn't she,
something that calls her this or that,
      for instance: 'cruel',
Yet couldn't exist without her cruelty.

        *

PS: This verse, it seems, contains the gist
        of tomes of learned
        philosophy,
        but it's much easier in it to detect the twist
        of such and such
        illogicality.

        Alas, the *dis*advantage is that our great find
        does not help much
        so long as there's an isolated *I*
        who talks
        and talks
        and talks
        about its mind.

ON A SHORT VISIT TO ALBION

> 'The cruellest lies are often told in silence'
> Robert Louis Stevenson

Between Folkestone and Dover
Grey clouds veil the cliffs
with silence.
Then the clouds vanish
and the cliffs are speechless.

DOWN THE RIVER

I saw the bent shoulders of the great old man
   as he turned round to buy fruit at the barrow,
I saw the furtive eyes in the white face of his old concubine,
And I knew they had sold my beloved
To the fraud with the bad breath.

...AERE PERENNIUS...

My poem
lasts
   no longer
than
   your perm.

INTEGRITY

When there is something to grieve over,
Grief is as healthy as joy—
when there is something to be happy about.

Crestfallen...

Crestfallen—
Pourquoi?
No answer.
All crystals have melted.

SEMPRE TUO

No? Well, if no then no
you're not the only big brother
who preaches one sort of comme-il-faut
and practises—quietly—another.

PIGEON'S SONG

U ́ – u u   u ́ – u   u ́ – u u   u

Catholics Protestants Jews Mohammedans...

Catholics Protestants Jews Mohammedans
Oh God, how thankful I am that I have never received any
    religious instruction
The first Bible I saw was the one I bought in 1938 from
    a Salvation Army Officer in a *boîte* in Paris
It was lost in the war
Today I have 4½ copies: one in English
                       one in French
                       two in Polish
                       and a half in Modern English
—an abomination committed by some who hate to admit
that it was STYLE that ennobled NONSENSE.

THE CATASTROPHE THEORY

The theory of the last straw
that broke the camel's back.

They say that all empty sets...

They say that all empty sets are equal
(sets with no elements)
therefore: there is only one empty set.

Logic is digital...

Logic is digital
intuition is analogue
as the world is analogue
intuition is often right
where logic fails.

An amateur thinks...

An amateur thinks
his triolet beautiful
because he broke a fingernail
on his typewriter's keyboard.
With a poet it's different,
if his poem is bad
even his broken heart
will not make it better.

Straight from my bed...

Straight from my bed, still warm, she hastens to a shop
To buy something she doesn't need. A tin of salt. A paper clip.
And I know the time will come
When it will be to me that she'll say: 'shopping'
When I ask her where she has been.

When women advise women...

When women advise women how to handle their men,
They forget their Shakespeare they forget their Bacon.
It is a clever giggle of an imbecile crashing a wine decanter
   with a hot electric iron,
And they think it's a Clausewitz
   taken from the top shelves of
their respective husbands.

Never will he be a writer...

Never will he be a writer, a person
who cannot understand that a man
can break into his love's house
to learn the truth about her lovers, and then go
to the kitchen, and not to the bedrooms,
for reasons of delicacy.

We are all of us guests on this planet...

We are all of us guests on this planet
And with guests—you know how it is
Some are nice and some are tiresome
And some behave as if they were hosts
and even as they die they believe
that they have owned the sun and the air and the history that took place
even before they were born.

Logically speaking...

Logically speaking
the fact that you can say
  Golden Mountain
doesn't mean that a golden mountain must exist,
but physically speaking
if you cannot formulate, let alone
  express something
without an 'α'
you accept the existence
  of the 'α'
until you find a way of expressing
what you want even
without using 'α'.

You said I told you things...

You said I told you things
without using words
You said I am a Zen master
without knowing it
That is what *you* said. I
really do not know what I know
without knowing it.

We dont't actually know...

We don't actually know what it means
'Poincaré's homunculus thinking'
if it is of the size of a molecule
or of the size of a galaxy.

When Mrs Eilmer says...

When Mrs Eilmer says:
'I'll come again on Friday, if God permits'—
she shows that she doesn't believe in the inevitability
of the recurrence of events.
She actually says:
'I'll come on Friday, if I come on Friday.'

England, table, Hamlet, and I...

England, table, Hamlet, and I
Got mixed together with minus π
Who will manage to set them apart
Politics, logic, science, or art?

THE MIDDLE IS

for Dom Sylvester Houédard

The *is* of ethics is the *is* of physics
But what is the middle is?
And what is the is in But what is?
And what is the is in And what is?
And what is
And what is
is?
Oh, the infinite regress of languages based on nouns!

For milliards of years I was not
then I started to happen
now—I am happening
and in a short while I'll stop happening
These are characteristics of a verb
not of a noun.
Am I a verb?

Alas
all backward paths
of thoughts
are doomed to lead to something presumed.
In a language based on nouns
    it will be a noun:
God   Big Bang   Biological Soup   Somethingness   Nothingness
In a language based on verbs
    it will be—perhaps—the middle is?

In films...

In films
verbs are static
they don't move
even such a verb as
to gallop is static
it doesn't move
it is the horses that move.

Freedom of speech...

Freedom of speech means that
governments have no right to
silence a speaker.
It does not mean that
his listeners have no right to do so.

There is a discrepancy...

There is a discrepancy between
law and justice.
When a black man is fined five shillings
for having made a row in a public house,
we see that the law takes its course.
But some of us don't feel
that justice has been done,
if we learn that
he made the row because he had been refused
a glass of beer by the publican.

I am qualified...

I am qualified to write about
killing, not because I have killed,
but because I was killed.
Both in science & in life
Evidence is still the best safeguard
against the miscarriage of truth
& the miscarriage of justice.

You may not believe me...

You may not believe me
But
When I have enough of it
for tomorrow's breakfast
(which nowadays is not
an exceptional event)
I do feel guilty.
Why should I?
Well,
Because
after a melancholy reflection
I think I have taken more
than I have given.
It is for me that
men get up at 5.30 am
and at 6.30 queue at the bus stop.

B.R. IN *MY* AUTOBIOGRAPHY

This is a chapter of *my* biography, not of his.
That is what it is meant to be, and that is how
I want you to read it.
                        In the world I was born into, he was already
part of nature.

History *is* an exact science...

History *is* an exact science
It teaches us that if it snows
for 2 days it stops snowing on the 3rd day
but if it snows for 3 days
it stops snowing only on the 4th day.

Mathematics is too important...

Mathematics is too important
        to be left to the mathematicians
they are too sophisticated in their techniques
& too naive in their way of seeing
        the world.

One of the effects...

One of the effects of
the artist's role in society is
that he must bite the hand that feeds him.

Non-understanding of this
is as common among the right
as among the left political wing,
the understanding—seems to be even
more rare on the left than it is on the
right.

I am most disliked...

I am most disliked by those who
preach what I practise.
Because I don't preach, or because they don't practise?

I adore the Immaculate Mary...

I adore the Immaculate Mary
because she didn't talk so much,
especially of love.
Whether Theotokos, or Christokos,
I adore her, because she didn't talk
so much, especially of love.

I am too-oo religious...

I am too-oo religious
If you see what I mean
to believe in anything
If you see what I mean

Not even in the Golden Calf
If you see what I mean
Not even in Karl Marx
If you see what I mean

That is why, why my friends
If you see whom I mean
both like me and dislike me
If you see what I mean

Because I'm too religious
If you see what I mean
to believe in anything
If you see what I mean

Not even in the Linguistics
If you see what I mean
of the anti-mystic mystics
If you see what I mean

That is why my enemies
If you see whom I mean
dislike both me and themselves
If you see what I mean

Because I'm too religious
If you see what I mean
to believe in anything
If you see what I mean

You asked me...

You asked me
to read to you
This invitation
so nice and flattering
made me go to a park and sit on a bench and reflect
made me walk through the streets and reflect
made me lie on my couch and reflect
and the reflection
both melancholy and not sad
was like the hand of a watch
moving round and round and round
always forward
and always coming back
to its point of departure.
Hence melancholy
because
questioning the essence of progress.

I wanted to grow a crystal
and bring it to you as a gift
I wanted to wrap it nicely in words
and give it to you tonight.

Alas
—and it is not that I'm not capable of putting forms in
    symmetries of rhymes and rhythms—
but crystals grow
from undisturbed tranquillity
and this I couldn't find in myself.

Thus
I got up from my bench
I stopped in the middle of the pavement

I jumped out of my dream:
What I shall bring you
is a flaming torch
a loudhailer
an Allons, Citoyens!

Fortunately
—and it is not that I'm not capable of putting rhymes and
   rhythms into a howling cry,
but—
having lived through hairpin bends of History
and met and seen and heard
some howling voices
both true and false
of which the former is more dangerous
—I called my sense of humour to stop me, just in time.

Thus

I have come to you to-night
empty-handed
having no offerings of Aims to give
Because no Aim is so exalted
that it be worth a heartbeat more
than Decency of Means.

Because
when all is said and done
Decency of Means
is
the aim
of aims.

THE AIM OF AIMS

Some naive lovers of semantics believe
that *if* only our leaders
(of all sorts)
could understand the meaning of their own pronouncements
they would amend their ways.
What an illusion!
They—the leaders—
know the mechanism of Language much better
than all the semanticists,
                linguistic philosophers,
                      & logical formalists put together.
It's only that they use their knowledge for their own purposes.
And when a Poet
        or a Novelist becomes a demagogue
the same applies to him.
Because POETRY as well as POLITICS may be morally *vicious*,
and intellectualy *dishonest*.
In such cases
both *Poetry* and *Oratory*
(political, religious, philosophical)
are like *Crime*.
The greater a Crime is
the more impressive it is
but the less excusable.
Thus
when all is said and done
one finds
that no poetic rhymes
and no politic aims
are more important
than decency of means.
Because
when all is said and done
decency of means
is
the aim of aims.

Said Robert Louis Stevenson...

Said Robert Louis Stevenson
in a letter to somebody
'I believe in the ultimate decency
of things.'

Well, in the World that God commanded
to consist of cells devouring cells
Decency of Means
is Man's
ultimate
evolutionary
Aim.

Why do you want to win...

Why do you want to win
silly fool
What a strange ambition!
Is that what they taught you at school:
Competition?

Is it nice to be the first in the race,
Is it kind to overtake other run-n-ners?
Don't you know that to win
shows not virility
but bad man-n-ners?

Put kind words...

Put kind words into your mouth
because the words will become thoughts
and the thoughts will become deeds
and the deeds will become masks
and the masks will become the faces of
the new generation.

'**Meet another philosopher,**' said Edith at Bertie's birthday party. So they agglamourated aground me, bgright twitching integrogation marks in their eyes: 'Where from? Where from? From where?', meaning: the womb of which Alma Mater feeds you with her milch juice for teaching young beasts what you have learned from old lizards, meaning: whom have you unsaddled, O unknown reptile; for the vacating of whose chair are you lying in wait, meaning: are we going to beg you to notice us, or is it you who are going to bbegg us to nnotice you; come on, quick, quick, this suspense is intolerable, quick quick tell us, quick, quick, because neither social intercourse nor academic evolutionary processes are possible without that bit of information; quick, 'where from? where from? from where?' 'From Erewhon,' I said. Their bristles, their quills, their fishscales hedgehogged. Tiny, miniature, electrically lit geographical globuses were turning round quickly in their searching eyes, Erewhat?, where was it? They tried to remember what geography they had learnt ten, twenty, thirty years ago at school. 'From *where?*' they repeated. 'From Nowhere,' I explained; and thought: if I deserved to carry the name of philosopher, which place to have come from would be more appropriate than a place which is independent of any longitude, or latitude, or altitude, or creditude, but I had no time to develop the thought because at this moment one of the blackjacketed teachers shoved forward his army,—and the wellgroomed stiff index finger, and the ring on it; and the hand, and the wrist, went through my chest, effortlessly, as if I were composed of the air that surrounded me. Which is as it must be, because if you come from nowhere then it is logically necessary that wherever you are you are nowhere, because if there were anywhere a borderline such that jumping over it could transfer you to this side of it, then nowhere would have to be on the other side of the borderline and, being there, it would be somewhere, which is not compatible with being nowhere, and thus, consequently, once you are nowhere, nowhere you are wherever you are, the only meaning of which is that you are indistinguishable from what is around you, pierceable by what what-is-around-you is pierceable by; if it is air then you are air, if you are submerged in water then you are water, if you are buried up to your armpits while your head is in the centre of a soundwave, then you are earth up to your armpits and a scream from your armpits up. The blackjacketed teachers made unequal numbers of steps backwards, three steps, one step, two steps, and the zaubercircle was no more a circle, it broke behind me and its loose ends globetrotted away to akimbo around another point on the parquet floor. Well, they had to be somewhere. They would feel lost anywhere else. It is only I who nowhere am lost and feel at home everywhere. I feel at home in any child's cot, in any woman's bed, in any corpse's coffin. I feel at home with viruses in the guts of a louse, and with lice in a dove's feathers, and with doves in the heart of Jesus. Goodnight chums. Goodnight everybody. Goodnight.

LAPSUS LINGUAE
or
DEATH OF A MAN OF LETTERS
AS SEEN BY THE ESTABLISHMENT OF ANONYMOUS MANDARINS

He's never been
he isn't
and he shall not
be.
We are as many with him
as we are without him.
You do not see him when you look at the place where he stands
What you hear is not what he's saying
What you touch is not at all him when you shake both his hands
Exclaiming: Dear Mr. Themerson, how nice to miss you again!

I am a priest...

I am a priest
I have my own religion
Nothing to do with any of yours.
I have one parishioner:
Myself.
But even he
comes and goes as he likes
Not frightfully faithful.

MEANING AND TRUTH

You inquire into meaning and truth
I inquire into you
he inquires into me
But meaning & truth don't inquire into him

Meaning & truth couldn't care less
and he drifts uninquired into
and drifting in his 10,000 ton heavy armour
he inquires into me
who inquire into you
who inquire into meaning and truth.

WHY IS THERE SOMETHING RATHER THAN NOTHING? (Rp 1974)

for John Archibald Wheeler

Feed one computer with the Strangeness of Existence
Feed another with the Strangeness of Nothingness
Send them both to a Registry Office
and wait
9
months.
And when the newone is born
screaming, kicking, refusing to give you the answer
turn round
and open the window.

FREAKS

1½ ≠ 2−½   is? are?

in physics...

in physics = mathematics works
             in calculating physical values.

in logic   = mathematics fails
             in calculating truth values
             because it manipulates
             elements as if they were
             things in themselves
             and in the world of facts
             nothing is anything
             without there being something
             else (no door is a door
             without there being
             a house somewhere).
             (If not in reality, then at least
               in the mind of the architect.)

Logicians compare sentences...

Logicians compare sentences
with sentences, Novelists
compare sentences with the
world.

Maths & logic...

Maths & logic
imposes upon the world its findings
even when it doesn't fit
even when logical proof
contradicts experimental evidence
(experimental evidence does not
constitute a proof).

To draw a white square...

To draw a white square on a white
sheet of paper, you have to use
ink that is not white.
Yet you can paint a whole square
on white painted canvas,
by giving it a different texture.

It is comparatively easy...

It is comparatively easy
to describe a falling stone, or a
bird flying, or a man who runs;
it is not easy to describe the same
stone, but motionless, or a bird, but
suspended in mid-air, or a man—standing.
Especially, if you don't know why
he should move, ever.

OPUS 132

I see a trawler faraway between my toes,
My heels deep in the sand,
And suddenly, like an unasked breakfast on a seaside tray,
A thought appears in front of me on the horizon
That Beethoven is not immortal, after all.

My childhood...

My childhood wasn't happy at all, though I thought it was.
I thought I was privileged. This mistake
Gave me a sense of human dignity,
And it took Nature fifty years to break it
Into a hundred bits of bones which now I gather
And stick together with some wry humility,
Choosing to mend the broken
and not bend the sane.

Where I go...

Where I go
and wherefrom I come
are not the same place.
Unless you take the road of my
                journey
and bend it, like a piece of wire,
                      into a circle.

LIFE-TIME

It takes a minute to count a minute
and the time spent counting doesn't count.

For *o* in *now* . . .

For *o* in *now*
n is a half-forgotten past
w—a half-foreseeable future

For *s* in present . . .

For *s* in present
one *e* is in a faraway past
the other in an unforseeable future.
How fast can you live
to be now ?

WHEN AND WHERE

The edge of the world is at walking distance,
the end of Time is on the face of the clock;
It is the next street,
    where our neighbour lives,
        that we need a car to go to.
It is *now* that will come 'Nevermore'.

PASSAGE OF TIME

A young poet told me,
(and I used to think the same when I was young),
That nothing is ever lost, somebody
is always there, and responds, and carries the heart of a poem within him,
perhaps to the other side of the world, and then,
perhaps in some twenty years,
recollects it.

The young poet doesn't know,
(and I didn't know when I was young),
how quickly   twenty   years   pass   by
and silence follows.

If a fairy asked me...

If a fairy asked me some 20 years ago,
did I wish to be great or good,
I think that
(drawing on my present day 'wisdom')
I would answer (however reluctantly)
good—and (again—drawing on my
present day 'wisdom') by good I wouldn't
mean anything grander than
harmless.

When one is seventy...

When one is seventy
One has seen trees growing
One is still scanning rhythms
But one doesn't search for rhymes
any longer.

When one is seventy
One has seen trees growing
And one misses
the giants one has survived.

Is this the right time...

Is this the right time to write a verse and look for a rhyme
            at the end of one's long life
When the proud pleasure of having penned & printed & published
            all those prose sentences
            pales & fades out?
Is this the right time to have more faith in the form
            than in the flesh of fiction
            and the facts of the flesh
And closing the argument by finding
            the proof not in the truth but in the rhyme?
Now, in which land are those promised rhymes
            to one's long life, to fades out, to the flesh,
            and to rhyme itself?

ON BEING TOLD OF BEING A FAILURE

I have no son,
I am the end-product.
If *I*'m not good enough,
This branch must be sawn off.

PROOF FOR DESIGN

I am too old. I have no more time
to write two hundred pages of prose.
Can I squeeze them into a few lines
of unrhymed verse
drawn across some green fields
and join them into a perfect circle?
A perfect circle is nothing but symmetry.
Perfect symmetry is perfect nothingness.
It is the dent on a kicked football
It is the flattening of the North and South Poles
It is the nose on a round head
that is the evidence of the cause.

I have hardly been...

I have hardly been
and
already
am on my way out.
Have hardly had time to grasp
the answer
to the question
how many questions
are unanswerable
how many answers
are questionable.
Have hardly had time to put
two bricks together.

To versify...

To versify
    not in the 1st person singular
—difficult.
And in the first—
    boring.
And anyway—
at your (old) age?
Ridiculous!
Neither: why
nor: what for.

CODA (OR ENVOI)
ON MY 70th BIRTHDAY

I didn't ask to be born
yet, when the chance occurred
the chance of a lifetime
I seem to have grasped it greedily (I bit my mother's breast
                                dangerously
                                and had to be given a wet nurse;
                                it's only now I realise
                                she must have had her own child
                                to be able to feed me).

Today
I do not ask to die
Yet as the time approaches
the very thought that I shall never know what will happen to those
                                I'll be leaving behind me
                                in the world which is
                                not at all prettier
                                not very much better
                              & not enough wiser
                                than it was three score & ten years ago,
makes me gasp for breath.

It is not enough...

It is not enough to pinch a rose
      in your neighbour's garden
to be called a thief.
It is not enough to scramble
      a couple of eggs
to be called a cook.
It is not enough to write a few lines
      rhymed or unrhymed
to be called a poet.
I am not a poet.
A poet writes his verse at the time of strength
I wrote these little bits
      at the time of weakness.

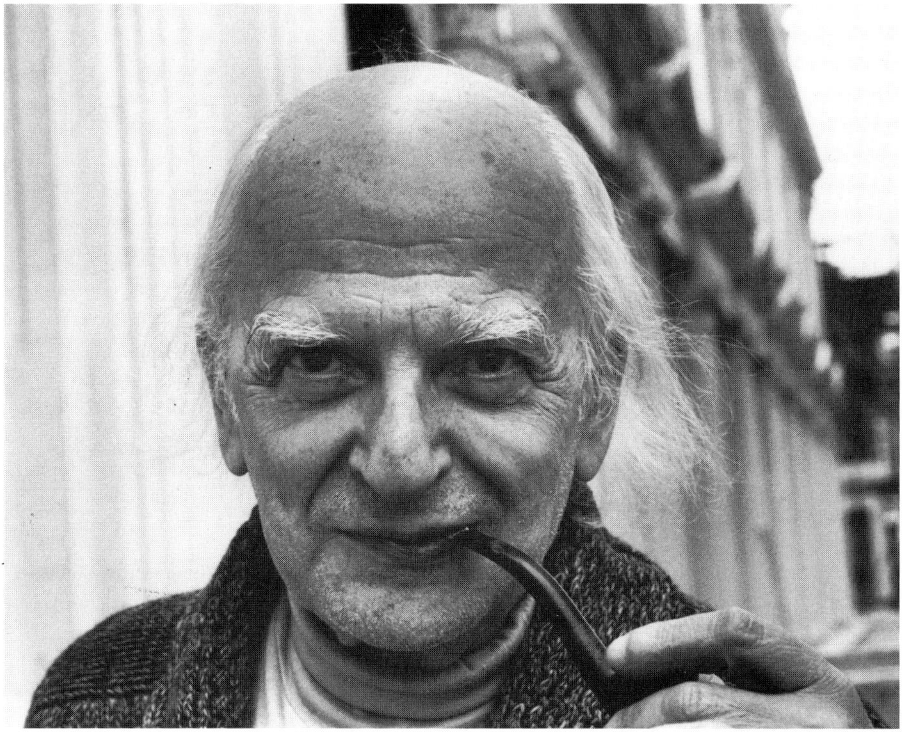

INDEX OF FIRST LINES
WITH TITLES
DATES
BIBLIOGRAPHY UP TO 1989
AND NOTES

A young poet told me... 150
PASSAGE OF TIME
An amateur thinks... 129
On Semantic Poetry, London, Gaberbocchus Press, 1975, p.14
Robert Nye (ed). *P.E.N. New Poetry I.* London, Quartet Books, 1986, p.168
And so they went... 110-111
CASTOR & POLLUX
prose poem
1954
Other Voices, vol.1, no.2, London, 28 January 1955, n.p.
Au travers de ma rivière... 48-53
LA RÉVOLTE DES OREILLES
(trilingual poem in six parts)
1942
Between Folkestone and Dover... 126
ON A SHORT VISIT TO ALBION
or A SHORT TRIP TO ALBION
c.1962
Poetry Review vol.65, no.4, London, 1975, p.383
Catholics Protestants Jews Mohammedans... 128
1986
'Come on, hand it over...' 18-21
part I
CROQUIS DANS LES TÉNÈBRES
Voiron, June 1941
Croquis dans les Ténèbres, London, 1944, pp.9-11, limited edition of 500, distributed by Hachette. Dedicated to Franciszka.
Barbara Wright's English translation is published here in full for the first time.
Crestfallen... 127

Djugashvili, Djugashvili... 113
  SOME YEARS AFTER HIS DEATH
  1960
Dost thou not know... 117
England, table, Hamlet, and I... 6, 131
  Robert Nye (ed). *P.E.N. New Poetry I*. London: Quartet Books, 1986. p.167
Enjoy your bath... 122, 123
  TO ENCOURAGE THE APPLICATION OF MATHEMATICAL METHODS TO HISTORICAL ANALYSIS
  several versions, including visual and vocal, June 1965
  visual & vocal versions in *WF 100*, Writers Forum, London, October 1973
Fascists and some anti-fascists... 115
  1960
Feed one computer... 144
  WHY IS THERE SOMETHING RATHER THAN NOTHING? (Rp 1974)
  for John Archibald Wheeler
  1974
  Saintly Fingers no.4 *(The Lycanthrope Quarterly)*,
  Newcastle-upon-Tyne, December 1975, n.p.
  [Dr J. A. Wheeler, theoretical physicist, Joseph Henry Professor Emeritus, Princeton University]
For *o* in *now*... 149
  Poetry Review vol.65, no.4, London, 1975, p.383
  Blank Page no.2, London, June 1989, n.p.
For *s* in present... 149
Freedom of speech... 133
  c.1962
Haida three large powerful... 62-63
  SEMANTIC POETRY TRANSLATION OF THE OPENING WORDS...
  1945
  included here is the first version which appears in Polish in
  Nowa Polska, vol. VI, no.2, London, February 1946, pp.108-109
  Bayamus. Poetry London, 1949, pp.62-63
  General Piesc i inne opowiadania, Warsaw, Czytelnik, 1980, pp.76-77
  all others begin with:
  Heigh my three large powerful...
  Bayamus, London, Gaberbocchus Press, 1965, pp.73-75

Poetry Review, vol.61, no.3, London, 1970, p.206
Concrete Poetry, Amsterdam, Stedelijk Museum, 171, p.88
as 'Shape Poem' in Eric Williams, ed. *Dragonsteeth*, London, Edward Arnold, 1972, p.31
On Semantic Poetry, London, Gaberbocchus Press, 1975, pp.33-35
Bayamus, Paris, Christian Bourgois, 1978, pp.88-91,
(French translation by Gérard-Georges Lemaire).

Having just had his tongue... 90
ELEGY IN A LONDON BUS
1951
New Departures 1, London, 1959, p.39
in Italian translation by Lorenza Bosco in
Il Caffè, vol X, no.3, Rome, June 1962, pp.52-53

He didn't wash his hands... 114
PILATE

Here they are, Sir... 116
P.M.

He's never been... 143
LAPSUS LINGUAE or
DEATH OF A MAN OF LETTERS
AS SEEN BY THE ESTABLISHMENT OF ANONYMOUS MANDARINS
1974
Poetry Review, vol.65, no.4, 1975, p.382
Palpi 20, London, September 1988, p.30

History *is* an exact science... 135

How nice it is... 60-61
SEMANTIC POETRY TRANSLATION OF A POLISH POPULAR SONG...
1945
Nowa Polska, vol. VI, no.2, London, February 1946, p.III-112
Bayamus, Poetry London, 1949, pp.68-69
Bayamus, London, Gaberbocchus Press, 1965, pp.80-81
On Semantic Poetry, London, Gaberbocchus Press, 1975, pp.40-41
Bayamus, Paris, Christian Bourgois, 1978, pp.95-97,
(French translation by Gérard-Georges Lemaire).
Generał Piesc i inne opowiadania, Warsaw, Czytelnik, 1980, pp.81-82

Hunger teaches you wisdom... 124
MILLION WAYS

I admire poets... 119
    1960
    Poetry Review vol.65, no.4, London, 1975, p.382
    Palpi 20, London, September 1988, p.30
I adore the Immaculate Mary... 136
I am a poor child... 17-18
    PETIT NÈGRE ÉCRIRE PETIT POÈME
    Marseille, 1941
    Croquis dans les Ténèbres, London, 1944, pp.7-8,
    see **'Come on, hand it over...'**
I am a priest... 143
    1973
I am in love with her hair... 43-47
    GRECIAN NIGHT
    Hôtel de la Poste, Croix Rouge Polonaise, Voiron, August 1941
    Croquis dans les Ténèbres, London, 1944, pp.31-35,
    see **'Come on, hand it over...'**
I am most disliked... 136
    c.1953
I am qualified... 134
    c.1953
I am too old... 152
    PROOF FOR DESIGN
    early 1960s
I am too-oo religious... 137
    16 September 1975
I am waiting... 91
'I can't get used to...' 21-24
    part II
    CROQUIS DANS LES TÉNÈBRES
    Voiron, June 1941
    Croquis dans les Ténèbres, London, 1944, pp.12-14,
    see **'Come on, hand it over...'**
    Published as **'The Poet and the Angel'**, *Comparative Criticism* no 12, Cambridge, 1990, pp.259-262
I can't read your poetry... 119

I didn't ask to be born... 154
    CODA (OR ENVOI)
    ON MY 70TH BIRTHDAY
    London, 15.1.1980
I don't read poetry... 118
I have hardly been... 153
I have no son... 152
    ON BEING TOLD OF BEING A FAILURE
    1962
I have studied the subject... 116
    LOVE OF NATIONALS
I know, I know, my friend... 34-39
    part V
    CROQUIS DANS LES TÉNÈBRES
    1941
    Croquis dans les Ténèbres, London, 1944, pp.23-27,
    see **'Come on, hand it over...'**
I liked the wedding-cake whiteness... 112
    ON THE RISE AND FALL OF THE ONLY CHRISTIAN CHURCH FOUNDED BY A WOMAN
    1960
    ['Mariawici'—a catholic sect established in 1893 by Felicja Kozłowska in Płock on the Vistula.]
    Aylesford Review, vol IX No 1, Maidstone, Autumn 1967, p.52
I never believed in Thee... 24-29
    part III
    CROQUIS DANS LES TÉNÈBRES
    Voiron, the nights of June 1941
    Croquis dans les Ténèbres, London, 1944, pp.15-19,
    see **'Come on, hand it over...'**
I saw the bent shoulders... 126
    DOWN THE RIVER
    1960
I see a trawler... 147
    OPUS 132
    1960
If a fairy asked me... 150

If I don't despair... 121
    c.1954
If only those few words... 9
In films... 133
in physics... 145
Is this the right time... 151
It is comparatively easy... 146
It is not enough to pinch a rose... 155
It is strange... 116
It's not for me to say so... 101
    LITANY IN ZED
    1949/50
    SEMANTIC SONATA, 3rd movement
    see **I've got a white rag...**
It takes a minute... 148
    LIFE-TIME
    1960
    New Departures 7/8, London, 1975, p.142
    Blank Page no 2, London, June 1989, n.p.
It would have been comic... 121
    1953
I've got a white rag... 94-108
    SEMANTIC SONATA, [in four movements]
    June 1949-October 1950
    [Sometimes referred to as SEMANTIC SONATA No.2, which was to be published in December 1950 in a limited edition of 387 copies, designed and printed by Anthony Froshaug. In the event only a prospectus was published.]
    Froshaug's typographic layout was used for the *Semantic Sonata* in *factor t*. London, Gaberbocchus Black Series No.8/9, 1956, pp.51-64.
    The Sonata also appears in *On Semantic Poetry*. London, Gaberbocchus, 1975, pp.47-57
    L'Ennemi 1980, Paris, Christian Bourgois, pp. 143-88, (as 'Sonate Sémantique' in French translation by Gérard-Georges Lemaire).
    This first section was sometimes given the title: SINCE THE FIRST DAY OF GENESIS
I've met a man... 91
    A SONG OF A FLEA

Jarry's Shakespearian horror comic... 120
A REGRETTO
FREE-CASSEE—a group of three poems
1953
Let it continue... 56-59
JE SÈME A TOUT VENT
1945
Nowa Polska, vol VI, no.1, London, January 1946, pp.53-55
Bayamus, Editions Poetry London, 1949, pp.47-49
Bayamus, London, Gaberbocchus Press, 1965, pp.51-54
Bayamus, Paris, Christian Bourgois, 1978, pp.61-64,
(French translation by Gérard-Georges Lemaire).
General Piesc i inne opowiadania, Warsaw, Czytelnik, 1980, pp.54-57
Logic is digital... 128
Logically speaking... 130
1960
Logicians compare... 145
Mathematics is too important... 135
Maths & logic... 145
'Meet another philosopher,'... 142
prose poem
Richmond early 1950s
Most complex most specialised...69-73
SEMANTIC POETRY TRANSLATION OF THE PRAISE...
1945
Nowa Polska, vol VI, no.2, London, February 1946, pp.109-111
Bayamus. Poetry London, 1949, pp.64-67
Bayamus, London, Gaberbocchus Press, 1965, pp.76-79
On Semantic Poetry, London, Gaberbocchus Press, 1975, pp.36-39
Bayamus, Paris, Christian Bourgois, 1978, pp.91-95,
(French translation by Gérard-Georges Lemaire).
General Piesc i inne opowiadania, Warsaw, Czytelnik, 1980, pp.77-81
My childhood... 147
1960
Times Literary Supplement, London, 5 March 1964, p.198
cryptonymously as Tomasz Woydyslawski

My poem lasts no longer...126
    ...AERE PERENNIUS...
Neither T.S. Eliot... 120
    ON THE POETRY OF MONOPLANES AND BATHYSPHERES
    FREE-CASSEE—a group of three poems
    1953
Never will he be a writer... 130
No? Well, if no then no... 127
    SEMPRE TUO
    1978
On the peel of this apple... 40-41
    part VI
    CROQUIS DANS LES TÉNÈBRES
    Croquis dans les Ténèbres, London, 1944, pp.28-29,
    see **'Come on, hand it over...'**
One of the effects... 136
Polska kaszkę warzyła,... 86
    (Poland cooked a pot of porridge...)
    1946
    AND no.5, Writers Forum, London, September 1969;
    also in A. Riddell, *Typewriter Art*. London Magazine Editions, 1975, p.103
    [based on a traditional Polish nursery rhyme, the text reads: 'Poland cooked a pot of porridge. She gave some to this one, some to this one, and some to this one. And she wrung the neck of this one.']
Praise be to... 78-85
    THE LAY SCRIPTURE
    OR, A DRAFT FOR A PREFACE TO A TEXTBOOK OF PHYSICS
    1947
    published, printed and typographically designed by Anthony Froshaug, London, in a limited edition of 120, June 1947, 16 pp.
    With a drawing by Franciszka Themerson.
    Generał Piesc i inne opowiadania. Warsaw, Czytelnik, 1980, pp.163-167
Put kind words... 141
Said Robert Louis Stevenson... 141
Shooting at doves... 87, 88-89
    ABRACADABRA
    c.1952

New Departures 1, London, summer, 1959, p.38;
Il Caffè, vol x, no.3, Rome, June 1962, pp.51-52,
(Italian translation by Lorenza Bosco);
folding typographic setting: *An Excerpt from a Code*, folder no.5, Downfield Press, England, September 1965
(limited edition with drawing by Franciszka Themerson).

Some naive lovers of semantics... 140
THE AIM OF AIMS
1976
recorded by ST for Greater London Arts Association, *Dial-a-Writer* telephone service between 2 and 8 May 1978.
Blank Page no 2, London, June 1989, n.p.
[Elsewhere the text appears as prose.]

Straight from my bed... 129
1962

Taffy was a male native of Wales... 75-76
TAFFY WAS A WELSHMAN
preceded by a children's poem which inspired this Semantic Poetry translation
1945
Nowa Polska, vol vi, no.2, London, February 1946, pp.112-113
Bayamus, Poetry London, 1949, pp.70-71
Bayamus, London, Gaberbocchus Press, 1965, pp.82-83
On Semantic Poetry. London, Gaberbocchus Press, 1975, pp.42-43
Bayamus, Paris, Christian Bourgois, 1978, pp.98-99
(French translation by Gérard-Georges Lemaire).
Generał Piesc i inne opowiadania, Warsaw, Czytelnik, 1980, pp.82-84

That little thing... 113
c.1950

The edge of the world... 149
WHEN AND WHERE
1960
New Departures, 7/8, London, 1975, p.142
Blank Page no.2, London, June 1989, n.p.

The fermented grape-juice... 65-68
SEMANTIC POETRY TRANSLATION OF THE CHINESE POEM:
'DRINKING UNDER THE MOON' BY LI PO

(preceded by the T'ang Dynasty poem 'Drinking under the Moon' by Li Po, translated into English by Winifred Galbraith)
1945
Nowa Polska, vol VI, no.2, London, February 1946, p.108
Bayamus. London, Poetry London, 1949, pp.60-61
Bayamus, London, Gaberbocchus Press, 1965, pp.69-72
'A typographical problem'. *WF Pamphlet 3*, London, December 1969, pp.69-72
Bayamus, Paris, Christian Bourgois, 1978, pp.84-87,
(French translation by Gérard-Georges Lemaire).
General Piesc i inne opowiadania, Warsaw, Czytelnik, 1980, pp.74-75
Poezja, vol XXII, no 4/5, Warsaw, April-May 1987, pp.61-63
Blank Page no 2, London, June 1989, n.p.

The *is* of ethics... 132
THE MIDDLE IS
(for Dom Sylvester Houédard)
6 March 1975
[Dom Sylvester Houédard, the concrete poet of Prinknash Abbey, Gloucestershire]

The king of Sweden... 112
c.1961
Robert Nye (ed). *P.E.N. New Poetry I*, London: Quartet Books, 1986. p.167

The sun was shining brightly... 54
A MES AMIS FRANÇAIS HABITANT L'AMERIQUE...

The theory of the last straw... 128
THE CATASTROPHY THEORY

The worst has already happened... 124
1978

There are there... 115
1962

There are more keys... 31-33
part IV
CROQUIS DANS LES TÉNÈBRES
1941
Croquis dans les Ténèbres, London, 1944, pp.20-22,
see **'Come on, hand it over...'**

There are two ways... 124
NOBODY KNOWS
1960

    Poetry Review, vol.65, no.4, 1975, London, p.383
    Palpi 20, London, September 1988, p.30
There is a discrepancy... 133
They say that all empty sets... 128
This is a chapter... 135
    B.R. IN *my* AUTOBIOGRAPHY
(B.R. is Bertrand Russell)
To draw a white square... 146
To versify... 153
U ː - u u ... 127
    PIGEON'S SONG
We are all of us guests on this planet... 130
    1987
We cannot comprehend... 121
We don't actually know... 131
'What cruelty!'... 121
    GOYA'S PICTURES
What is it that he wants... 109
When I reflect on Nature's cruelty... 125
    c.1975
    Robert Nye (ed). *P.E.N. New Poetry I*, London, Quartet Books, 1986, p.169
When Mrs Eilmer says... 131
    c.1954
When one is seventy... 151
    25 January 1980
When there is something to grieve over... 127
    INTEGRITY
    1960
When women advise women... 129
Where I go... 147
Who created Thee who... 114
    HOLY VIRGIN
    1943
Why do you want to win... 141

Words about words... 107
   1949-50
   in Herbert Spencer. *Worte, Worte, Worte*. Cologne, Verlag Galerie Der Spiegel, 1972, n.p.
   SEMANTIC SONATA, see **I've got a white rag...**,
You asked me... 138-139
   introduction to a reading
   the ending is a repetition of the ending of THE AIM OF AIMS
   see **Some naive lovers...**
   see also **I knew you would dial this number...**
You inquire into meaning and truth... 144
   MEANING AND TRUTH
   June 1965
   Robert Nye (ed). *P.E.N. New Poetry I*, London, Quartet Books, 1986, p.168
You may not believe me... 134
You said I told you things... 131
You sentimental bastard... 120
   TO HEINRICH HEINE
   FREE-CASSEE—a group of three poems
   1953
$1\frac{1}{2} \neq 2-\frac{1}{2}$ **is? are? 144**

Index of titles

ABRACADABRA 87, 88-89
...AERE PERENNIUS... 126
A MES AMIS FRANÇAIS HABITANT L'AMERIQUE... 54
A MILLION WAYS 124
A REGRETTO 120
A ROUNDELAY
    ON THE NARROWNESS AND UNEXPANDABILITY OF WORDS 99
    (title given to 'sugar is soluble in water...'
    —see SEMANTIC SONATA)
A SONG OF A FLEA 91
B.R. IN *my* AUTOBIOGRAPHY 135
CASTOR & POLLUX 110-111
CODA (OR ENVOI)—ON MY 70TH BIRTHDAY 154
CROQUIS DANS LES TÉNÈBRES
    the group of poems under this title 15-47
    the main poem 18-41
DOWN THE RIVER 126
ELEGY IN A LONDON BUS 90
FREAKS 144
FREE-CASSEE—a group of three poems 120
GOYA'S PICTURES 121
GRECIAN NIGHT 43-47
HOLY VIRGIN 114
INTEGRITY 127
JE SÈME A TOUT VENT
    SEMANTIC POETRY TRANSLATION OF THE QUARTIER LATIN FRENCH SONG 56-59
LA RÉVOLTE DES OREILLES... 48-53
LAPSUS LINGUAE OR
    DEATH OF A MAN OF LETERS
        AS SEEN BY THE ESTABLISHMENT OF ANONYMOUS MANDARINS 143
LIFE-TIME 148
LITANY IN ZED 101
LOVE OF NATIONALS 116
MEANING AND TRUTH 144
NOBODY KNOWS 124

ON A SHORT VISIT TO ALBION or A SHORT TRIP TO ALBION 126
ON BEING TOLD OF BEING A FAILURE 152
ON THE POETRY OF MONOPLANES AND BATHYSPHERES 120
ON THE RISE AND FALL OF THE ONLY CHRISTIAN CHURCH FOUNDED
    BY A WOMAN 112
OPUS 132 147
PASSAGE OF TIME 150
PETIT NÈGRE ÉCRIRE PETIT POÈME 17-18
PIGEON'S SONG 127
PILATE 114
P.M. 116
PROOF FOR DESIGN 152
SEMANTIC POETRY TRANSLATION OF A POLISH POPULAR SONG... 60-61
SEMANTIC POETRY TRANSLATION OF THE CHINESE POEM:
    'DRINKING UNDER THE MOON' BY LI PO 65-68
SEMANTIC POETRY TRANSLATION OF THE OPENING WORDS
    OF A RUSSIAN BALLAD 62-63
SEMANTIC POETRY TRANSLATION OF THE PRAISE OF CREATED THINGS WHICH
    ST FRANCIS MADE WHEN THE LORD CERTIFIED HIM OF HIS
    KINGDOM 69-73
SEMANTIC SONATA 93-108
SEMPRE TUO 127
SINCE THE FIRST DAY OF GENESIS 94-98
    (title sometimes given to the first movement of SEMANTIC SONATA)
SOME YEARS AFTER HIS DEATH 113
TAFFY WAS A WELSHMAN 75-76
THE AIM OF AIMS 140
THE CATASTROPHE THEORY 128
THE LAY SCRIPTURE
    OR, A DRAFT FOR A PREFACE TO A TEXTBOOK OF PHYSICS 77-85
THE MIDDLE IS 132
TO ENCOURAGE THE APPLICATION OF MATHEMATICAL METHODS
    TO HISTORICAL ANALYSIS 122-123
TO HEINRICH HEINE 120
WHEN AND WHERE 149
WHY IS THERE SOMETHING RATHER THAN NOTHING? 144

LIST OF ILLUSTRATIONS

All drawings are by Franciszka Themerson, unless otherwise indicated

p.5	*Stefan Themerson*, 1942
p.6	Manuscript of *England, table, Hamlet and I*
pp.8, 13	Drawings by Stefan Themerson, 1982
p.14	*Nuit de Ténèbres*, 1942, from the 'Unposted Letters'
p.16	*Croquis dans les Ténèbres*, linocut, c.1943
p.30	*Stefan's Escape*, 1941, from the 'Unposted Letters'
p.42	*Cauchemar Grec*, 1941, illustration to *Croquis dans les Ténèbres*
p.55	Untitled drawing, 1963
p.77	Illustration to *The Lay Scripture*, linocut, 1947
p.87	*Abracadabra—An Excerpt from a Code*, a folding typographic setting
p.92	*Stefan Themerson*, 1940
p.109	*Sancta Providentia!*, 1941, from the 'Unposted Letters'
p.156	Stefan Themerson, 1987

From Stefan Themerson's collection of quotations:

> 'Just before she died she asked, "What is the answer?"
> No answer came. She laughed and said,
> "In that case, what is the question?" Then she died.
> Those were her last words,
> but they say what she had always been saying.'[1]

---

[1] *Gertrude Stein—A Biography of Her work* by Donald Sutherland. Yale University Press, 1951, p. 203